DEMCO

HOW
YOU
TOO
CAN
TEACH

Reading Text

of a Basic Training Course

for Church School Teachers

By ALLAN HART JAHSMANN

General Secretary of Sunday Schools

The Lutheran Church — Missouri Synod

CONCORDIA LEADERSHIP TRAINING SERIES

CONCORDIA PUBLISHING HOUSE · SAINT LOUIS, MISSOURI

CONCORDIA LEADERSHIP TRAINING SERIES

FIRST SERIES

Old Testament History: A Survey of the Old Testament — Arthur W. Klinck

New Testament History: A Survey of the Life of Christ and the History of the Apostolic Church — William F. Arndt

Fundamental Christian Beliefs: A Survey of Christian Doctrine — William F. Arndt

The Life of Saint Paul, the Greatest Missionary — William F. Arndt

Home Life in Bible Times: A Study in Biblical Antiquities — Arthur W. Klinck

The Story of the Church: A Brief History of Christianity — Theodore Hoyer

Our Church and Others: Beliefs and Practices of American Churches — Lewis W. Spitz, Sr.

SECOND SERIES

Teaching in the Sunday School: The Teacher's Position and His Work — Theodore J. C. Kuehnert

Learning to Know the Child: An Introduction to Child Psychology — Adolph Haentzschel

Teaching Little Amalee Jane: How the Small Child Learns the Way — Allan Hart Jahsmann

Evangelism in the Sunday School: Training in Soul Winning and Soul Keeping — Elmer A. Kettner

Teaching the Word to Adults: A Course for Adult Bible Class Teachers — Harry G. Coiner

For information on course credits and certificates awarded on completion of these courses, write to the Concordia Leadership Training Office, 210 North Broadway, St. Louis 2, Missouri.

THIRD PRINTING 1965

Concordia Publishing House, St. Louis 18, Missouri

Concordia Publishing House Ltd., London W. C. 1

Copyright 1963 by Concordia Publishing House

Library of Congress Catalog Card No. 63-18733

MANUFACTURED IN THE UNITED STATES OF AMERICA

INTRODUCTION

This text is intended primarily as background reading for prospective and beginning Sunday school teachers who are in a basic training program. A trainer's manual which presents a design for such a program is available from the publisher of this book. The manual offers suggestions and materials for at least twelve class sessions and also outlines a period of apprenticeship and supervised student teaching. Completion of the course leads to a Certificate of Acceptance into the Fellowship of Church School Teachers, a vast body of dedicated servants of Jesus Christ.

Though introductory in scope, this textbook deals with the basic task and concerns of all who are engaged in the teaching ministry of the church. Also pastors and experienced or even professional church school teachers will find a fresh study of the fundamentals of parish education stimulating and rewarding. This book begins with theological reasons for teaching, draws on the latest insights of the social sciences for ways of teaching, and bases its hopes on the Spirit of God for greater power and success in teaching.

Grateful acknowledgment of counsel in the preparation of this course is due the members of the Leadership Training Committee: Pastor Herman Etzold, Dr. A. C. Mueller, Dr. Theodore Kuehnert, Pastor Howard Kramer, and Dr. Donald Deffner. The training manual was field tested experimentally in St. Louis, Mo., and Topeka, Kans.

The author's hope is that the Lord of the church, our Savior Jesus, will bless the study of this book. May it serve to multiply greatly the number of Christians enlisted into the teaching ministry of His church and may it give to those who enter this service some essential training for their task.

ALLAN HART JAHSMANN

CONTENTS

Page

INTRODUCTION

CHAPTER ONE   7

The Educational Task of the Church

The Church Designed by God
The Mission of the Church
The Parish Education Program

CHAPTER TWO   14

A Look at Learning

When Have I Learned Something?
Ways in Which People Learn
Teaching That Leads to Change

CHAPTER THREE   22

The Spirit, the Word, and the Teacher

God's Spirit and God's Word
God's Word and God's Spirit
God's Church and Its Teachers

Page

CHAPTER FOUR   33

The Pupils and Their World

Learning to Know Our Pupils
The Worlds in Which They Live
Age-Group Characteristics
Uncovering Personal Concerns

CHAPTER FIVE   42

The Teacher and the Class

Types of Group Leadership
Conditions That Affect Group Spirit
Furthering the Group Process
A Concluding Reminder

CHAPTER SIX   51

Teaching Methods and Techniques

Sharing and Doing Methods
Telling and Sharing Methods

CHAPTER SEVEN   60

Preparing to Teach a Lesson

Lesson Planning Procedures
The Purposeful Use of Materials
Constructing a Lesson Plan

CHAPTER EIGHT   69

Concerns Beyond the Classroom

The Teacher as Evangelist
The Teacher as Counselor
The Teacher as Teacher
The Teacher as Student

CHAPTER ONE

THE EDUCATIONAL TASK OF THE CHURCH

Focus of the chapter: **The why and what of Christian education in the light of the nature and purposes of the church.** Reading time: about 20 minutes.

Every good teacher gives attention to *what* he is to teach and *how* he might try teaching what he wants to teach, but first of all he is aware of what is to be accomplished in terms of a *why* and *wherefore*. Educators speak of this why and wherefore as the purpose, objective, goal, aim, or desired outcome of a program or activity. Purpose gives direction and meaning and drive and value to what one does in general as well as in a specific lesson.

It is necessary, therefore, to begin with some consideration of the ends which the Sunday school or any other church school is to serve. And since any program of Christian education is to serve the purposes of God for His church, a brief review of the nature and mission of the church may help to clarify what the educational task of the church is.

The Church Designed by God

Many Biblical terms highlight the nature of the church, i. e., the church designed by God. Though we might use the word church to refer to a building or an organization, the Scriptures identify the church as "the body of Christ," the body of which Jesus Christ is Head and Lord and in which all believers in Him are members (Rom. 12:4, 5). In this sense there is only one church of God, only one Christian church, "one body and one Spirit . . . one Lord, one faith, one baptism, one God and Father of all. . . ." (Eph. 4:4-6)

The Greek word *ecclesia,* or church, means a fellowship or community of people who have been chosen and "called out" from among many for some special purpose. So again, "the church of God" is the sum total of people who have been chosen and "called out" from the world by God to life with Him and service to Him. They are "the people of God" (1 Peter 2:9, 10), "the household of God" (Eph. 2:19), in which God is the heavenly Father and all its members His children.

The children of God are in a covenant relationship with God, a covenant of mercy and adoption established by God through the life, death, and resurrection of Jesus Christ. Because human beings enter this covenant relationship through faith in Jesus Christ, the church is also called "the household of faith" (Gal. 6:10), and its members are called followers of the Lord (1 Thess. 1:6). These followers of Jesus Christ have their sins washed away (forgiven) and the robes of their lives washed white in the blood of the Lamb (Rev. 1:5; 7:14). Therefore they are called "saints," the holy ones (Eph. 4:12), and together they are "the communion of saints," the redeemed, the sanctified, the beloved of God, and the blessed.

There are many other words and phrases with which the Bible portrays and characterizes the church fashioned by God.* But one more particular perspective deserves special mention here. The communion or fellowship of the community of saints (the holy, universal Christian church) is a "fellowship of the *Spirit"* (Phil. 2:1), a "communion of the Holy Ghost," a fellowship "with

* Paul S. Minear discusses 95 such images in *Images of the Church in the New Testament* (Philadelphia: Westminster Press, 1960).

the Father and with His Son, Jesus Christ" (1 John 1:3), through the workings of the Spirit of God.

Apart from the Holy Spirit there can be no Christian faith and life with God and no people of God (1 Cor. 12:3). Therefore the body of Christ, the church, is seen individually and collectively also as a spiritual temple, Zion, built out of living stones in whom and among whom the Spirit of God lives. (1 Cor. 6:19; 1 Peter 2:5)

The Mission of the Church

What reason does God have for building His church? Why does He call and gather His people out of spiritual darkness into the marvelous light of His mercy in Christ Jesus? Why does He enlighten and sanctify and keep them with Jesus Christ in the one true faith by giving them His Spirit?

Peter says, "Ye are a chosen generation, a royal priesthood, an holy nation, a peculiar people, *that ye should show forth the praises of Him who hath called you out of darkness into His marvelous light*" (1 Peter 2:9). The glorifying of God is and ought to be the ultimate purpose of everything the church is and does, collectively and individually.

Now, how is God glorified? In the Holy Scriptures the saints, the redeemed, are called to be faithful to God as was their high priest Jesus Christ (Heb. 3:1-3), to bear His image in righteousness and true holiness (Eph. 4:24), to walk in good works (Eph. 2:10), to be "an habitation of God through the Spirit" (Eph. 2:22), to serve God by loving and serving fellow human beings (1 John 4:12), to glorify God by being salt and a light in the world. (Matt. 5:13-16)

But God's name is hallowed, His kingdom comes, and His will is done on earth only as men receive His Spirit and enter into covenant relationship with Him through acceptance of His mercy, peace, forgiveness, and fellowship. Because this life and salvation is received through faith in Jesus Christ (Acts 16:31) and this faith is created and nurtured by the Word of God (Rom.

9

10:17), it is necessary for the church to preach the Gospel, to witness to what it knows and believes about Jesus Christ, to baptize, to make disciples of the Lord Jesus, to teach them all things He has commanded.

To define the life and work of the church, the Bible uses many words and pictures. Note how they all have in common the ministry of the Word. In Matt. 13:3-9 Jesus describes the work of His kingdom as the sowing and cultivating and harvesting of seed. The seed, He says, is the Word of God. In Matt. 20:1-7 Jesus compares His kingdom, the kingdom of God, to a vineyard, the lord of which said to all standing idle in the marketplace: "Go, work in my vineyard." Paul and Peter talk about the work of the ministers or servants of God as the stewardship of the grace and mysteries of God (1 Cor. 4:1, 2; 1 Peter 4:10, 11). The resurrected Jesus told Peter that love of Him was to be expressed in the feeding of His lambs and sheep. (John 21:15-17)

Regardless of whether one speaks of the mission of the church as missions or education, as evangelism or Christian nurture, as preaching or teaching, it always involves the proclaiming, the offering, the sharing, the explaining, the showing, the teaching of the grace of God in Christ Jesus to other people. And always the hope is that they will accept this grace and grow in it and become mature, active Christians.

In Ephesians Paul speaks of this task as "for the perfecting of the saints, for the work of the ministry, for the edifying (the building up) of the body of Christ, till we all come in the unity of the faith . . . unto the measure of the stature of the fullness of Christ" (Eph. 4:12, 13). This equipping and building up of its members for service is the immediate central concern of the church, according to Paul, and it is for this work that Jesus gave the early church apostles, prophets, evangelists, pastors, and teachers and continues to give to His church pastors, teachers, and other servants of the Word to carry out the preaching and teaching mission of the church. (Eph. 4:11)

The Parish Education Program

The next question is, How can and does the church witness and preach and teach and nurture and build up the body of Christ? We have already suggested that it does this when its members individually and collectively fulfill their calling to be Christians and thereby glorify God in what they are and in whatever they do. But this "being Christian" is first of all a *spirit*. The *spirit* of the church in the home, in interpersonal relations, and in its organizational life either furthers or inhibits the sanctifying work of God's Spirit and is of first importance. Church schools and church school teachers, too, will nurture others spiritually only as they participate in the Spirit of God.

But the Spirit of God, we have acknowledged, works through the Word of God. The seed of life with God is the Word. This Word is the means of grace. So a congregation provides for the ministry of the Word in its midst by calling pastors to preach and to teach the Word and to administer the sacraments, the visible Word, in its behalf.

However, the work of the church is so many-sided that a large and diversified ministry is needed even in a parish. A congregation provides for a fuller ministry of the Word when it establishes various church schools and educational programs and calls additional leaders and teachers, full-time or part-time, professional or nonprofessional, to do this work of equipping the saints and building up the body of Christ officially in its behalf.

These leaders and teachers of parish schools and youth and adult education programs need to be, first and foremost, teachers of the *Word,* because, you see, the purpose of parish education in any form ought to be the same as the purposes of the church. A church school is simply an agency by which a church attempts to fulfill its mission. It must never be an end in itself, an organization that exists for its own sake and for purposes in conflict with the mission of the church.

Furthermore, the task or ministry of a *lay* leader and teacher is no different from that of a *professional* minister and teacher

11

of the church. It is only the scope of responsibility and the particular functions that vary. And much is required of *anyone* who wants to serve his Lord and his church in the public ministry of the Word.

Of great importance is the teacher's own study of the Word. The amount and kind of Bible study a church teacher engages in will determine the spiritual worth of his teaching more than anything else he might do. Even though content of Christian teaching is indicated by the curriculum and course materials, the teacher is the final determiner of the kind of theology that is actually taught. Therefore he must have a proper understanding of the Christian faith.

In addition to many other considerations, a Christian teacher must also be aware of his task in terms of his pupils and their Christian development: "Till we all come in the unity of the faith and of the knowledge of the Son of God unto a perfect man, unto the measure of the stature of the fullness of Christ" (Eph. 4:13). But what are some of the characteristics of a well-developed, mature Christian? What are some of the distinguishable features of the desired end product and therefore the specific objectives of any parish program of Christian education?

A little reflection will soon suggest that the first mark of a well-developed, well-rounded Christian is personal faith in Jesus Christ, his Lord and Savior. But a healthy Christian is further characterized by (1) growth in Bible knowledge, (2) ability to apply knowledge to problems of human life, (3) participation in the life and work of the church, (4) a rich devotional life, (5) a sense of personal stewardship and of Christian vocation, and (6) a readiness to contribute to Christian social action in his community and in the world at large.

All of these aspects of a Christian portray the kind of person God wants His church to nurture. They embrace most of the desired outcomes of any program of Christian education.

To those who had received faith in the righteousness of Jesus Christ the apostle Peter wrote: "Grace and peace be multiplied unto you through the knowledge of God and of Jesus our Lord. . . . And beside this, giving all diligence, add to your faith virtue, and to virtue knowledge." Then, after mentioning a number of other marks of Christian character and personality, he continues: "For if these things be in you and abound, they make you that you shall neither be barren nor unfruitful in the knowledge of our Lord Jesus Christ. But he that lacketh these things is blind and cannot see afar off and hath forgotten that he was purged from his old sins." (2 Peter 1:2-9)

To put it theologically, justification and sanctification are inseparably related. Therefore the task of Christian education is the nurturing of Christian persons who will live in keeping with their Christian faith in all aspects of their life. This requires a great and never ending parish education program. But in the extent of its fulfillment lies the fulfillment of the purpose of the church. To this task you are called.

REVIEW QUESTIONS

1. How many Biblical terms for the church of God can you name?

2. Why do we need to keep in mind God's design for His church in order to understand properly the educational task of the church?

3. To what are the saints, the redeemed of God, called in the Scripture?

4. What must the church do in order to develop and equip the saints for their work of service?

5. What is the proper relationship between the church and its educational agencies?

6. In terms of the end product, what are the major specific objectives of parish education?

CHAPTER TWO

A LOOK AT LEARNING

> Focus of the chapter: **The nature of the learning process and the kind of teaching suggested by the ways in which people learn, particularly when the concern is the Christian nurture of the individual and the spiritual building up of the body of Christ.** Reading time: about 20 minutes.

The first chapter called attention briefly to what the church's teaching task is in terms of what God desires His church to be. To become what God wants His people to be, they must learn to know Him as He revealed Himself in the person, work, and teachings of Jesus Christ.

But this knowledge must be a knowledge of the heart as well as of the head. Needed for life with God is a faith created and directed by the Spirit of God working in the spirit of the individual. Such a personal, vital faith, which confesses that Jesus is the Son of God and Savior of the world (1 John 4:14, 15), grasps the blessings He has earned for all by His life, death, and resurrection and sanctifies or forms Christian character from within.

Such faith expresses itself by its own power in Christian love and good works, and only the Spirit of God working through Christian faith can develop a genuine Christian personality and life. However, Paul wrote: "We are to grow up in every way into Him who is the head, into Christ" (Eph. 4:15 RSV). To

14

this end also the learning of the will of God and its applications to life become important. It is folly to assume that people with faith in Christ need no instruction and training.

Having considered in a general way *what* the members of a church school need to learn, let us give some thought to *how* human beings are most likely to learn. Particularly are we interested in how Christians might grow up to be *mature* Christians, the kind of people God wants them to be. With this in mind, let us first look at what learning is.

When Have I Learned Something?

There are many definitions of learning. Some people see learning mainly as the acquisition of *intellectual* knowledge. A learned man, from this point of view, is one who knows a great deal about a subject or, better still, about many subjects. People who value this kind of learning tend to place much emphasis on memorizing. For them one has learned what one can remember. And the child who can recite back or give "right" answers "knows" and has learned his lesson.

Others see learning chiefly as ability to do — the acquiring of skill. For them the hallmark of education is *training,* and so they emphasize learning by doing. Such education is useful but tends to develop technicians rather than wise men. In religious education those who hold this view stress the values of learning *how* to pray or *what* to say and *how* to study the Bible and *what* verses to use and *when*. But they may have little interest in helping others gain basic understandings and appreciations.

And then there are those who think of learning mainly as adaptation — learning how to get along, how to solve problems, and how to adjust. In this "school" of thought much stress is placed on thoughtful trial-and-error activity and on "thinking through" and "thinking out" problems, especially social problems. This kind of learned person can see connections and draw proper conclusions and can see ahead and act intelligently. His learning centers on ability to *think* — in a practical sort of way.

Still another view of learning says: "I know deeply only that which I feel." Though this learning usually involves some insight and may be enriched by insight, it is basically personal, emotional experience. "I can't explain it; I just know it's true; something inside me tells me so." This something inside me — whether intuition, a sensitivity, or an aesthetic response — seems to flow from or consists in attitudes, interests, value judgments, and appreciations.

This kind of learning is usually underrated but is essential to the enjoyment of life and personal fulfillment. "Whatever is true, whatever is honorable, whatever is just, whatever is pure, whatever is lovely, whatever is gracious, if there is any excellence, if there is anything worthy of praise, think about these things," says the Bible (Phil. 4:8 RSV). Of course, this isn't the only kind of learning the Bible recommends.

Each one of the different kinds of learning mentioned has merit in its own right. Intellectual knowledge is needed. The Scriptures lay great emphasis on knowledge of God and His truth. Furthermore, knowledge develops into truer understanding through doing and experience. How can a person learn to love except by loving, to pray except by praying, to give except by giving? Likewise, unless there is meditation and a "thinking through" of the implications and applications of one's faith, knowledge is likely to remain static. And when appreciation of all that is good and beautiful is lacking, also the Christian life lacks breadth and richness.

But even though any general statement of learning must include all the previously mentioned types, there is one concept of learning that is especially important in Christian nurture — the view that learning involves change and growth. Teachers and pupils alike are to grow toward spiritual maturity, and growth occurs through changes — changes in ways of thinking, changes in emotional responses, changes in outward behavior.

Learning in the sense of growth is "becoming." From this point of view the little child "learns" to walk and talk and "learns" how to be a grown-up. Growth in understanding is seeing things differently or feeling them more appropriately and deeply. Mature behavior is expressing in words and actions what one thinks and feels. Applied specifically to Christian growth, this definition underscores the fact that a person truly learns the Christian faith only to the extent that he puts off his sinful nature and moves into a new life with God in Christ. In other words, his learning becomes realized and real only as it changes him.

Ways in Which People Learn

The usual discussion of how people learn deals with teaching techniques rather than with the broad question of what furthers human development. For example, in *The Ladder of Learning,* Victor Hoag estimates that people of all ages may remember only 5 percent of what they hear, 10 percent of what they see, 20 percent of what they repeat, 40 percent of what they say in their own words, perhaps 50 percent of what they read, 60 percent of what they discuss in a vital group, 75 percent of what they do or make, and fully 95 percent of what they teach. These estimates are loose, debatable opinion.

We are here concerned not just with remembering but with methods which are most likely to bring about change in human beings — in their character and personality, in their being and behavior. On this question, especially the science of psychotherapy has a great deal to say.

The first factor essential to any successful treatment of a psychiatric patient is the patient's own motivations and expectancies. In order to have any promise of change and improvement, a patient must "hurt," he must be in distress, he must want to change, and he must want to change because of a conviction that his emotional sickness brings with it a living death. In Christian nurture, too, the learner needs constantly to be reminded of the "living death" of separation from God and the necessity of being in fellowship with God in order to be transformed by His Spirit.

The pupils must want to change. They won't change unless they want to.

A second prerequisite to human change demonstrated by psychotherapy is that the patient must have not only the desire but also the expectation of help. He must have the hope of healing. In Christian nurture the use of the Law is important for developing an awareness of the *need* for forgiveness and new life with God, but always the emphasis needs to be on the positive Gospel promises of the grace and power of God in order that hope may burn brightly in the pupils — hope for the life and salvation Jesus came to give.

A third major factor in human change is the relationship between the patient and the doctor. There is some indication that this is the common element in the success of various types of psychiatric treatment. This relationship must be one of basic trust. The patient must see the therapist as a person who can help him, and the therapist must believe that he is able to help the patient. Also in Christian education the pupil must have a basic respect for the *teacher* as one who can and will help him. Even Jesus was unable to influence people who rejected Him.

And teachers, too, must believe that their pupils — every last one of them — can become something they are not. The child who feels that his teacher has given up on him will also very likely give up caring and trying, but many a person has been changed by an awareness of someone else believing in him.

So it appears that the development of a helpful relationship between teachers and pupils is vital to learning if learning is to result in changes in the lives of the pupils. This positive personal relationship is established and enhanced by what is called "the accepting role of the therapist." In order to encourage the patient to communicate the deep emotional attitudes which govern his behavior, the therapist religiously follows a pattern of nonjudging acceptance of the patient.

A great deal needs to be said about acceptance as a method

of treatment or of teaching. It is subject to much misunderstanding. It is a means for the betterment of a person, not an end. Its purpose is to permit an honest spiritual communion between individuals or the members of a group and their leader in order to deal with *real* thoughts and feelings. It is not condoning or merely absence of condemnation. It is respect for the other person's right to express himself (whether child or adult) and interest in his welfare without attempts at manipulating or molding him.

The development of a close personal relationship between a teacher and his individual pupils is important for still another reason. When in the process of what is called identification a pupil "identifies" with his teacher, the teacher becomes *"my* teacher," the school and church *"my* school and church." And this identification, in turn, leads to incorporation of the loved object or features of it into the self. Whether the principle is absolute or not, common observation will verify that the pupil who identifies with his teacher through affection, admiration, and submissiveness will "take into himself" not only what the teacher believes and teaches but also what he is and does. This underlines the importance of the teacher being a model of Christian character.

Another principle of learning on which there is common agreement is that a person's emotions must be involved in a process if it is to result in personality change. In other words, *feelings* are essential to a transforming experience.

Education, also Christian education, has tended to regard formal verbal communication of knowledge as a chief means of establishing faith, loyalties, and behavior. But also in education the meaningful involvement of the learner in a learning process requires a stirring of his emotions, since they provide the power or motivation for change of behavior.

In *Christian* personality development, too, this principle applies even though the Spirit of God is the source of Christian faith and life. An individual has a living faith only as the Spirit of God enters into the spirit and life of the individual. And feeling is an element of life and spirit.

Teaching That Leads to Change

Obviously the ways in which people learn suggest the ways to teach, since teaching has as its purpose the furthering of learning. And when the desired learning or ends are changes in human beings, the question of effective teaching is determined by the kind of procedures that result in change.

Some of the principles underlying personality change and development have already been indicated. It remains for us to look at a few more, mainly from the angle of teaching.

Because personal involvement of the learner (his heart and life) is necessary if significant learning (learning that makes a difference) is to take place, a good teacher attempts to arouse and uncover the inner, personal thoughts, feelings, and experiences of the learner. This, of course, must never be done for its own sake. The purpose is to relate the life of the learner to that which is to be learned.

In Christian education it is the Word of God which indicates what is to be learned. But here the point is that this Word is more likely to speak to the learner and get a hearing, is more likely to be relevant and meaningful, when the learner is encouraged to identify and discuss the issues in the Word in reference to his own thoughts, feelings, and behavior. Even little children like to "think and tell."

This suggests a related principle of teaching that has become a truism but is still not seriously taken into account by most educators, namely, the principle of personal participation. This is the fundamental fact that no change, and therefore no real learning, takes place within a person without the participation of the person. Therefore the participation of the pupil at the deepest possible levels of personal experience must become the concern of the teacher who desires to influence others more than superficially with his teaching.

Obviously not all activity is on a level of personal involvement. It can be very superficial and impersonal. In education much activity that has been labeled pupil participation (learning by doing) is more in the nature of "busy work." Such activity in Christian education fails to confront the learner with an issue and a word from God and the challenge to express his own responses to God in his own way.

The principle of participation, which the philosopher Martin Buber calls "the act of inclusion," requires ways by which the learner will have opportunity to make that which is to be learned his own. When the learner is led to relate himself to a matter, he comes to know it personally and in his very being, where it is more likely to make a difference in his life.

Does all this really apply to Christian education and training in which the Spirit of God alone can regenerate (convert) and transform? What about the Word of God, which is the seed of life and the means of grace? Isn't it the only essential concern — "the one thing needful" — in Christian nurture? Let us consider this question in the next chapter. It is a vital issue.

REVIEW QUESTIONS

1. What are some types of learning that may not affect the learner's spirit or life?

2. How would you answer the question, When has a person truly learned something?

3. What are some of the necessary attitudes of the pupil in order that learning may take place?

4. Why is a positive emotional relationship between teacher and pupil important for learning?

5. What is meant by the principle of personal participation?

6. How does acceptance by the teacher and the group serve to involve the learner on the level of personal participation?

CHAPTER THREE

THE SPIRIT, THE WORD, AND THE TEACHER

> Focus of the chapter: **The related functions of the Spirit of God, the Word of God, and the people of God in the processes of Christian education; also the responsibilities of a teacher of the church.** Reading time: about 25 minutes.

After looking at various conditions that seem to enter into learning understood as change of thoughts, feelings, and behavior, one might ask: "But where does God fit into this operation? Doesn't the Bible teach that in Christian education everything depends on God? And if so, isn't my job simply to teach the Bible?"

To answer such questions, one must have a proper understanding of the relations between the Spirit of God, the Word of God, and the teachers of the Word of God. For such understanding one must consider the respective *functions* of the Spirit, the Word, and the people of God. It will then become evident that for Christian nurture to take place, the three cannot be separated.

God's Spirit and God's Word

The Word of God came to the prophet Zechariah in the symbolic dream of a sevenfold candlestick with an olive tree on either side. When in the dream the prophet inquired about its meaning, an angel explained by answering: "Not by might nor by power but by My Spirit, saith the Lord of hosts" (Zech. 4:6). The successes and blessings of God's church and kingdom are dependent entirely, in the final analysis, not on organization or programs or any other human force, but on the activity of God's Spirit and therefore on God Himself.

This essential need of the Spirit of God for life with God and the enjoyment of His gifts extends to every individual member of the church as well as to every human being not yet in the church. "No man can say that Jesus is the Lord but by the Holy Ghost" (1 Cor. 12:3), and this is true no matter how many Bible stories and Bible verses and Bible doctrines and prayers and other religious practices one has learned. A man (or woman or adolescent or child) can know the Bible well and still not have saving faith in Jesus Christ. The devils even believe that the Bible is true, but are not saved by such faith. (James 2:19)

This basic truth the church dares to ignore only at the risk of her life, and the church's leaders and teachers are foredoomed to spiritual failure, regardless of other accomplishments, unless they take this doctrine seriously. "Truly, truly, I say to you," said Jesus to Nicodemus, who knew his Bible very well, "unless one is born of water and the Spirit, he cannot enter the kingdom of God" (John 3:5 RSV). And Paul said by inspiration: "It is God which worketh in you both to will and to do of His good pleasure." (Phil. 2:13)

The Spirit of God is essential to Christian conversion, renewal, and sanctification because of the nature of man. In many passages the Bible speaks of man as a sinner, as carnal (ruled by sensual desires), as dead in trespasses and sins (Eph. 2:1), as hostile to God and His will (Rom. 8:7). "So then," Paul concludes, "they that are in the flesh cannot please God" (v. 8), but "as many as are led by the Spirit of God, they are the sons of God." (V. 14)

Next question: How can human beings receive the Spirit of

God? Here we need to note first another great truth often forgotten, namely, that the Spirit of God is not subject to human command. Nor can His operations be contrived, guaranteed, and taken for granted, not even by the use of the Bible and religious symbols, traditions, and instructions — much less by rules and regulations, admonitions and exhortations.

Always the Spirit of God is a gift of God — *sola gratia* — alone by grace. "By grace are ye saved *through faith,*" and this is the next point to remember. The Holy Spirit, the Spirit of God, enters and becomes a quickening force in human life in the process of Christian faith, not apart from faith. When Peter reported to the other apostles that God had given the Holy Spirit to the gentiles just as He had to them, he said that God purified their hearts "by faith" (Acts 15:9). "Ye are all the children of God *by faith* in Christ Jesus." (Gal. 3:26)

"God was in Christ, reconciling the world to Himself, not counting their trespasses against them" (2 Cor. 5:19 RSV). He *has* reconciled us to Himself (v. 18). But still the apostle Paul beseeches: *"Be* reconciled" (v. 20). And it is *through faith* in Jesus Christ that a human being *is* reconciled to God and receives His love and forgiveness. As the theologians put it, faith appropriates, lays hold on, God's forgiveness of sins and eternal life with God.

In the *accepting* of God's love in Christ (which is what the Bible refers to by the term faith) the believer also receives a new spirit (Rom. 7:6) and the mind of Christ (1 Cor. 2:16). And in becoming "a new man" renewed in the spirit of his mind (Eph. 4:23) the Christian becomes a person who walks "in newness of life" (Rom. 6:4). But all this is brought about by the Spirit of God working "through faith" in Jesus Christ.

Therefore the answer to the question of how human beings receive the Spirit of God lies in the means by which faith in Jesus Christ can be implanted and nourished in the human mind and heart. "How shall they believe in Him of whom they have not heard?" asks Paul (Rom. 10:14). And he concludes, "So then faith cometh by hearing and hearing by the Word of God." (Rom. 10:16)

The Bible speaks of this Word of God as "the power of God unto salvation" (Rom. 1:16), as "spirit" and "life" (John 6:63), as an "incorruptible seed" which possesses the power of spiritual regeneration (1 Peter 1:23), and as the Word which is able to save souls (James 1:21). Lutherans therefore call the Word the means of grace because it is the means by which the Spirit and grace of God are not only proclaimed but also conveyed.

God's Word and God's Spirit

To understand why the inspired writers of Holy Scripture can ascribe the same effects to both the Spirit and the Word of God, one must be clear on the Biblical concept of the Word. This understanding also may indicate the function which the people of God and particularly the teachers of the church have in the educational task which only God can accomplish.

In the fullest sense of the term, Jesus Christ is the Word — the revelation of God. John repeatedly calls the person Jesus the Word of God, the Word incarnate (John 1:1-12). Everything that He was and said and did on earth was a revelation of God. The Spirit of Christ is the Spirit of God, and the Bible often refers to both interchangeably. "The Lord (Jesus Christ) is that Spirit." (2 Cor. 3:17)

Second, the message of God's plan of salvation, of the redemptive work of Jesus Christ and God's forgiveness of sins, of peace with God and life with Him, is called the Word of God. It is the Word of the Gospel which on occasion is also called "the Word of Christ" (Col. 3:16), "the Word of reconciliation" (2 Cor. 5:19), "the Word of salvation" (Acts 13:26), "the Word of His grace" (Acts 20:32), "the Word of life" (Phil. 2:16), and many other terms which refer to the *message* of Christ's redemp-

25

tive work and God's offer of pardon, peace, and life with Him through Jesus Christ.

This message can have many forms and can be conveyed in many ways. To Zechariah it came in the form of a dream image. In the sacraments it is in the form of sacred acts involving specified elements. In the parables of Jesus the Gospel message is in a story. Preachers present it in the form of a sermon. Painters may present it in pictures. Parents and teachers can communicate it in conversations or discussions with their children.

Third, also the Bible is the Word of God. The Bible is the Word of God not only because it communicates the message of the Gospel but because "no prophecy of the Scripture is of any private interpretation . . . but holy men of God spake [and wrote] as they were moved by the Holy Ghost" (2 Peter 1:21). They wrote "not in the words which man's wisdom teacheth, but which the Holy Ghost teacheth" (1 Cor. 2:13). This is the doctrine of inspiration.

This divine inspiration extends to every word of Scripture. *"All* Scripture is given by inspiration of God" (2 Tim. 3:16), and *because* it is the Word of God, every word of Scripture is related to Christ and life with God through Him. To the two men on the road to Emmaus Jesus said: "O fools and slow of heart to believe all that the prophets have spoken. . . . And beginning at Moses and all the prophets, He expounded unto them in all the Scriptures *the things concerning Himself."* (Luke 24:25-27)

Luther, too, saw that all Scripture, rightly understood, is the revelation of the Gospel of Jesus Christ in the broad sense of the term and the communication of Jesus Christ Himself. "I see nothing in Scripture except Christ," said Luther. "All histories in the Holy Scriptures, when rightly viewed, have to do with Christ." (Weimar Edition of Luther's works, 4, 153)

In this view also the Law of God is in the service of the Gospel. The proper function of the Law is to develop a consciousness of

26

sin and the need for the Savior. It also sets forth the particulars of a life with God under the Gospel. But as Victor Bartling has demonstrated in a well-documented Biblical study of the term Word of God: "In the phraseology of the New Testament at least, Word of God is the name for the saving Word of the Gospel, to the exclusion even of God's Law, which is nowhere dignified by this distinctive title."

When Scripture communicates Jesus Christ, it is a means of grace and a channel of God's Spirit. But the use of words from the Bible outside the context of the Gospel does not necessarily convey the Spirit of God. Even the devil can quote the Bible to serve his ends.

Luther pointed out the need for presenting the written Word in terms of Christ and His Gospel when he wrote:

> . . . it is not enough just to take the life and work of Christ, and, in preaching [or teaching], merely to tell the story and the chronicle of events. . . . But He should and must be preached in such a way that, in both you and me, *faith* grows out of, and is received from, the preaching [and teaching]. And that faith is received and grows when I am told why Christ came, how man can use and enjoy Him, and what He has brought and given me. This takes place whenever a proper explanation is given of that Christian freedom which we have from Him: how we are kings and priests with power over all things; and how everything we do is well-pleasing to and granted by God. For when our heart hears about Christ in this way, it must rejoice through and through. It then yearns for Christ, receives consolation, and loves Him in return. "The Freedom of the Christian" in *Reformation Writings of Martin Luther,* trans. Bertram Lee Woolf, I (New York: Philosophical Library, 1952), 368.

God's Church and Its Teachers

There is still another way in which God reveals and communicates His Word and Spirit, namely, when His church or people live His Word, individually or in groups. To the Corinthians Paul wrote: "You show that you are a letter from Christ delivered by us, written not with ink but with the Spirit of the

27

living God, not on tablets of stone but on tablets of human hearts." (2 Cor. 3:3 RSV)

To the extent to which God's Word is lived, every Christian is a revelation of the Word and is, in the well-known expression of Luther, a little Christ. As a group, too, the members of Christ's body exemplify and make manifest the Word and Spirit of God especially when they love their fellowmen (1 Cor. 13). Messages and meanings are communicated by human personality and behavior as well as by words — by what we are and do as well as by what we say.

But even though all Christians express their faith and teach the Word (or fail to) by what they are and do, the public (official, formal) teachers of the church have some special responsibilities, tasks, and functions. What is the job of the Christian teacher? What is the church school teacher's role?

We could look back at the educational concerns of the church and make these the purposes of the teacher, for the church teacher must serve the purposes of the church in order to fulfill his purposes. But here let us rather look at the question in terms of actual classroom teaching — in terms of the *functions* of a church school teacher.

1. *Human Relations*

First there is the necessity of establishing and maintaining a relationship with the pupils, individually and as a class. Without contact, both psychological and physical, there can be no communication, and without communication there can be no positive learning of any kind.

Some of the principles involved in good teacher-pupil and teacher-class relations were indicated already in Chapter 2. Others will be considered in Chapter 6. Here let us simply note the *need* for developing good relations with our classes as a whole and with our pupils individually if we hope to teach them anything.

Furthermore, since spiritual nurture (growth of Christian faith and life) takes place only through the experience of the Holy Spirit, it is highly important that the relations between teachers and pupils be channels of God's Spirit. At least they ought not *grieve* the Holy Spirit of God (Eph. 4:30). Real Christian learning is most likely to result through *Christian* relationships and activity.

2. *Group Order*

Obviously a teacher cannot teach unless he has attention. Therefore a necessary part of his task is to establish a degree of order or control. In other words, there must be some discipline. Because of the sinfulness of human nature, this discipline is often lacking within the pupils and must therefore be instilled or imposed by the teacher.

Discipline is a major problem for some teachers. The absence of the problem is considered a mark of a good teacher. But in a church school a teacher might have strict control and poor discipline, because the question is whether the discipline is conducive to Christian learning. The answer to this lies entirely in whether the discipline is Christian and whether it serves to communicate the Word and Spirit of God.

3. *Motivation of Pupils*

The best discipline, of course, is that which comes from within the learner. The word discipline is related to the word disciple, one who is a learner and takes hold of the teachings of another. When pupils are personally engaged in learning, they are interested and attentive and self-controlled, and their behavior, though intensively active, is proper and not a problem. Another major concern of teachers, therefore, is the motivation of pupils in the direction of learning. No one learns unless he wants to.

Since Christian motivation is the working of the Spirit of God within the spirit of the learner, it cannot be forced by rules and rituals. It cannot even be induced except through the Word —

particularly the Gospel and the presence of Christ Himself. Because the Spirit of God works through the Word of God, pupils are motivated (directed and moved) by God when they are confronted with the Word of God and experience it through faith in Jesus Christ.

4. *Transmission of Content*

If Christian teaching and learning is to take place, the Word of God must somehow be transmitted. Transmission does not necessarily mean telling or drilling, as so many Christians are prone to think, even though these are basic methods. Today a good teacher realizes he can transmit the Christian heritage in a great variety of ways. But regardless of the method, the basic concern is "showing to the generation to come the praises of the Lord and His strength and His wonderful works that He hath done." (Ps. 78:4)

The importance of Biblical content in Christian teaching is underlined by what the psalmist continues to say in Psalm 78: "For He established a testimony in Jacob and appointed a law in Israel, which He commanded our fathers that they should make them known to their children that the generation to come might know them, even the children which should be born, who should arise and declare them to their children, that they might set their hope in God and not forget the works of God but keep His commandments and might not be as their fathers, a stubborn and rebellious generation, a generation that set not their heart aright and whose spirit was not steadfast with God." (Vv. 5-8)

5. *Pupil Participation*

The principle of participation was mentioned previously as a key to learning. Pupil participation leads to better teacher-pupil relations, personal motivation, and more effective transmission of content because it steps up attention, interest, personal involvement, and the meaningfulness of a lesson.

This being the case, a major task of the teacher is to plan learning activities that will require active pupil participation. Most nonprofessional church school teachers fail to see this aspect of their work. Because of its importance, much emphasis in this course will be placed on the use of sharing and doing methods.

6. *Pastoral Care and Guidance*

Though a teacher is not the pastor of an entire congregation, a Christian teacher must also be a pastor — a shepherd, an overseer — in the Biblical and functional meaning of the word. He is to care about and care for the souls of the individuals in his care. The concern of the church and of its teachers is the perfecting of the saints, the nurturing of spiritual growth toward Christian maturity in those who receive the righteousness and Spirit of Christ by faith.

This means that what a pupil does outside the classroom is as much a concern of the Christian teacher as what a pupil says and does in the class — perhaps more so. It means that the teacher must think in terms of the pupils as well as in terms of the lesson content. His job is to relate the two, and this isn't accomplished simply by starting with a prepared lesson and making an application. There is also the possibility of beginning with an incident or problem of life and relating it to the lesson, and there is the need for having the entire lesson speak to the pupils.

Summary

It is quite evident that there is much more to Christian teaching than a mere telling of Bible stories and the drilling of memory verses, even though these activities have their place. Spiritual teaching and learning is dependent on the Spirit of God working a change in the spirit of the learner. This is most likely to happen when members of the body of Christ are Christian teachers who communicate both the Word and Spirit of God through all their dealings with their pupils.

REVIEW QUESTIONS

1. How would you describe the relation between the Spirit of God and the Word of God?

2. Why is it important to keep a distinction between the functions of the Word of God and the Spirit of God even though their effects are identical?

3. What does the Bible mean by the term "Word of God"?

4. What is meant by the word "faith"?

5. In what way does a human being become "a letter from Christ"?

6. What do you think should be the major concerns of a Christian teacher?

CHAPTER FOUR

THE PUPILS AND THEIR WORLD

> Focus of the chapter: Some of the ways of learning to know the pupils, the major characteristics of the culture in which they live, the commonly identified age-group characteristics, and the need for uncovering and dealing with the concerns of the individual pupils in order to make teaching relevant. Reading time: about 25 minutes.

A few years ago much was written about the developmental concept of learning. This is the theory (1) that teaching is most likely to be fruitful when the learner is ready for it and therefore (2) that planned learning experiences must not be far beyond or beneath the individual's growth and development, even though they need to be challenging. In other words, instruction and training given too early may be harmful or at least wasteful, and lessons given too late may be unnecessary or incapable of stimulating the learner to further growth.

To illustrate, it would be folly to try to teach an average six-month-old child to walk or a six-year-old to work trigonometry problems. Likewise in religious education it would be inappropriate to teach a group of energetic youngsters the hymn "A Rest Remaineth for the Weary." At the other end of the scale, there would be little point in having a group of senior citizens in a rest home discuss the sexual problems of adolescents.

All this is simply to indicate the importance of grading instruction to the needs of the group and, better still, to the needs of the individuals in a class. Grading, in turn, requires that a teacher learn to know his pupils in general and, as much as possible, also as individuals. Especially for Christian nurture and Christian character development is it necessary that the teacher be able to identify and uncover the spiritual needs and concerns of his particular pupils, each one of whom is unique.

Another reason why it is so important that teachers get to know their pupils personally is that the Word and Spirit of God are to be communicated to the *pupils*. This requires that the Word be translated into present-day and personal terms. If this is not done, our teaching of the Word is likely to be irrelevant, pointless, not pertinent, meaningless, or at least unsuitable for those to whom it is directed. This being the case, the pupils are likely to be uninterested, not open to the message of the lesson, emotionally uninvolved, and therefore untouched by it.

Learning to Know Our Pupils

Whether we teach or will be teaching preschoolers, older boys and girls, adolescents, young people, or adults, there are a number of ways we can learn to know them better. We can talk to them and listen to them when they talk to us or to others. We can read books and pamphlets and articles about them. We can observe them. We can visit them in their homes. We can make an amateur case study of each individual in our class by collecting information and keeping notes about him.

For a general understanding of our pupils, we will want to become aware of various principles of human growth and behavior. Today psychology can be very helpful, especially to the teachers of the church whose primary interest is the nurturing of the *inner* life of their pupils. The following are but a few of the many insights to be gained from the scientific study of human beings:

1. *Every person is a unique human being with his own special gifts given to him by God.*

2. *Every individual has his own pattern and rate of growth and may therefore differ widely from others of the same age.*

3. *A human being develops as a total person and behaves as a whole or unit. His physical, mental, emotional, social, and religious "sides" are all interwoven, and all of these affect his soul or spirit, which is indivisible.*

4. *The growth and behavior pattern of a person usually is consistent and continuous; that is, it proceeds at an orderly rate unless unusual conditions play on it.*

5. *Every person has certain emotional needs which must be satisfied in some way, and the ways in which they are satisfied affect his Christian faith and life.*

The most commonly recognized emotional needs of human beings are the need for love and acceptance, the need for security, the need for self-respect and a feeling of worth, the need for freedom, the need to love and serve others, and the need for purpose and meaning in life. All of these deserve to be discussed at great length. Here the point is that the Word and Spirit of God, in relationships as well as in informal instruction, can speak directly to these human needs and will more likely do so when the Christian teacher addresses the Word to the anxiety, conflicts, guilt feelings, fears, loneliness, resentment, and hopelessness of the pupils or whatever their problems may be.

The Worlds in Which They Live

We can grow in the understanding of our pupils also by getting to know the world and the private worlds in which the pupils live. The culture, the times, the neighborhood, the kind of home, school, and church all contribute toward making a person what he is. People in America think and act differently in many respects than do the people of China or Africa. Modern Americans differ considerably from those of 100 years ago. The people living in Long Beach, Calif., differ distinctly in spirit and speech from a native inhabitant of Brooklyn, N. Y., or Biloxi, Miss.

The American child today is in a rapidly changing world. It is characterized by (1) East-West conflict and world tension; (2) economic specialization and stepped-up education, (3) media of mass communication moving children and youth into an adult world long before they are ready to handle it, (4) revolution in transportation, (5) many families on the move and increased urbanization, (6) materialism and what the editor of *Time* calls a decline in Puritanism, a freedom from conventions and codes of thought and behavior which can lead either to secularism or to creative, more vital, and personal Christian faith and life.

More important are the influences of the home, school, and church, but the effects of these, too, are determined by their qualities or spirit. Healthy children can survive a changing social scene if they have parents who accept and direct them in love and transmit to them the eternal spiritual truths of God's Word. By bringing them up "in the discipline and instruction of the Lord" (Eph. 6:4 RSV) parents anchor their children in the Rock of their salvation. Obviously the extent and quality of Christian instruction and training our pupils receive in their homes and church experiences will make a difference in their background and lives.

Age-Group Characteristics

We have noted that all pupils are individuals with their own unique heredity and background of experiences. But granting individual differences, human beings at a particular age level or stage of development tend to have characteristics in common. A growing understanding of the characteristics of a particular age level can help a teacher to communicate more meaningfully and successfully with pupils of that age group.

There is a great difference between teaching a nursery class effectively or a class of senior high school students, or a group

36

of adults, even when the subject is religion. There are important differences between three-year-olds and five-year-olds, between young teens and older teens. In the scope of this chapter we can look only at some larger groupings, and that but briefly. Learning to know the pupil is a continuous process.

The Preschooler

The Nursery class children (age 3) are generally not yet socialized to any extent and are often emotionally very attached to a limited number of people. They think and play more in isolation than in cooperation with others and often are very self-willed, because at this stage they are establishing themselves as individuals. They are not yet ready just to sit and listen to a teacher for any length of time, for their attention span is short. They enjoy physical movement, are interested in new sensory experiences (sights, sounds, feelings of touch), readily imitate others, but lack control of their emotions and behavior.

The Kindergarten (ages 4 and 5) continues to have a very limited experience and vocabulary, and teachers of this age group cannot assume that pupils know what they are talking about. Depending on early home training, they will have some awareness of Jesus and His church and some training in prayer, but the need and enjoyment of sensory experiences and repetition are still great. Time and distance and symbolism still mean very little to the child of this age, but he believes almost anything anybody tells him. He has a great deal of energy and remembers well what he learns. His imagination is very active even though he still thinks literally and concretely. Not as self-centered as the Nursery child, he is ready for some group worship, work, and play.

Primary and Junior Groupings (Grades 1 to 4)

Again the differences between a six-year-old in the first grade and a nine-year-old in the fourth deserve specific attention, but here we can only refer to them in general.

The child in the Primary department enjoys learning to read

and write, and his reasoning powers are awakening. He likes to communicate, especially with older people, and wants to be big, not little. He is beginning to establish friendships and is usually eager to please his teachers. His imagination is developing, but he often finds it difficult to express in words what he thinks and feels. He is still much more concerned about the present than about the future and quite unconcerned about moral and religious questions except as these relate to present and immediate situations.

Junior children in grades 3 and 4 (ages 8 and 9 or thereabouts) are in the midst of a so-called latency period, during which interest in parents or children of the opposite sex is at its lowest ebb. This permits a lot of serious mental as well as physical activity and a general preference for close friends of the same sex. The middle grader, for reasons related to the repression of the sex drive, often becomes highly compulsive and ritualistic. For example, he becomes a collector, one who must arrange his collections in perfect order. He is ready for the beginnings of independent and more detailed study and wants to understand and be given facts rather than expressions of emotion. Though he often appears to be matter-of-fact and uninterested in affection, he is intensely hungry for love and sometimes resorts to infantile behavior to obtain it.

Older Boys and Girls

The pupils in Preteen and Junior High departments (upper grades, ages 10 to 13) could be classified in various kinds of groupings. It must be remembered that these classifications overlap. Some 13-year-olds will be advancing into flowering adolescence while others will still be physically and emotionally in late childhood.

During this period girls grow faster than boys, and both acquire knowledge more readily than understanding. This stage of human development offers increased opportunity for intense intellectual development. Here peer-group relations (especially with close friends) begin to be more important than relations with parents and teachers, and boys in particular begin to strive for manliness with more daring than caution. Hero worship is quite common, and the gang spirit continues with one member of the group often becoming the accepted leader.

The High School Student

Many educators prefer to make a division between later childhood and early adolescence around age 12. This accounts in part for the Junior High grouping in some community and church school systems.

The early adolescent in general is in another period of rapid physical development and takes on an attractive, grown-up appearance. During this time he becomes physically very active, with an excessive appetite, but his intense physical growth and activity also run into fatigue, which adults sometimes wrongly interpret as laziness. The teen-ager's mental development, too, is reaching new heights, and he can no longer be taught as a child. He wants *reasons* for his faith and likes to argue. Many in this period become idealistic, dedicated to causes, and emotionally zealous.

Socially the teen-ager wants to belong to a clique, is again attracted to the opposite sex (this time of similar age), becomes interested in his personal appearance to the point of parental despair, is trying to find his place in society, and has a desire to help others and to amount to something. Religiously he now appreciates abstract discussion, symbolical ritual, and personal challenges to action, especially in behalf of causes.

Uncovering Personal Concerns

Self-evidently this discussion of age-group characteristics could be much more extensive. Teachers of young people and adults will find more elaborate studies of their age group in other books. Because of the limitations of space, we shall proceed to another major way of learning to know our pupils, namely, that of uncovering and discovering their personal worlds. Even more significant than the environments in which they live externally are those inner worlds of assumptions and attitudes through which our pupils perceive the world around them and receive the meanings of whatever is taught to them.

Understanding what is on the minds and in the hearts of the pupils helps the teacher to establish a sympathetic contact and relates teaching to the interests, concerns, problems, and needs of the learner. This, in turn, makes the educational process more timely, more relevant, more significant, more vital.

But how can a teacher "get at" the deeply personal lives of his pupils in order to apply his subject matter or lessons directly to them? There is no simple formula. The whole art of teaching is embraced in the answer. Some hints appeared in the discussion of how human beings learn; others will be considered in the study of methods of teaching.

But this much can here be said again: Whatever will lead a pupil to "open up" and express his own thoughts and feelings will help the teacher to relate his teaching to the experiences, concerns, and needs of the pupils in terms of personal references and applications. And whatever applications of lesson truths are seen and felt and expressed by the learner are more likely to be meaningful and accepted by the learner than those experienced only by the teacher.

REVIEW QUESTIONS

1. How will knowing the pupils (their age-level characteristics, family life, the world in which they live, their interests, experiences, thoughts, and feelings) help one to be a better teacher of God's Word?

2. What are some ways one might learn to know his pupils?

3. What are some predominant characteristics of life in America today?

4. How would you describe the particular age group you teach or intend to teach?

5. Look at a given Sunday school lesson and indicate what you think might be some of the applications to the lives of a specified age.

6. Ask someone in your chosen age group to tell you what his experiences, opinions, questions, feelings, and plans are in regard to the central thought or doctrine of the lesson you have selected.

CHAPTER FIVE

THE TEACHER
AND THE CLASS

Focus of the chapter: **The kind of classroom situation, group spirit, and teacher-pupil relations that are most conducive to communicating spiritual truth and experience; also the classroom role of the teacher who facilitates group procedures and group learning.** Reading time: about 25 minutes.

In the writer's *What's Lutheran in Education?* a chapter on "The Educational Function of Relationships" ends with the following conclusions:

1. The church of Jesus Christ finds its true spirit and nature in its relationship to God, and God relates Himself to the church through His Spirit of love (which found its highest expression in the life and death of Jesus Christ for the sins of the world). Furthermore, the Spirit of God in the hearts of His believing and redeemed people relates these members of Christ's body not only to their Head but also to one another. It places upon them the demands of love also in their relationships to their fellow men outside the church. Hence Lutheran education must consider as paramount a development of Christian human relations — among persons, within groups, and among groups.

2. Though Lutherans maintain that human beings are born again spiritually through the Spirit of God working in believers a new life in Christ by means of Baptism and the Word of God, they must also recognize that the supporting power of a Christian

environment is highly important to the growth and development of "the new creation" that stems from the seed of Christ and His Word. Some are convinced that it is only in a quality of life provided by a Christian group that a person can move toward Christian maturity. Whether this is true need not be debated. The truth is that ordinarily the transformation or sanctification of the personality of the individual believer in Christ is hindered or enhanced by his interpersonal and group relations.

3. Since a major objective of Christian education is the cultivating of Christian character and personality toward emotional and social maturity in Christ, it is highly important that Lutheran education give due emphasis to the need for a truly Christian environment, especially in the home, school, and church. For example, when a child fails to experience the forgiving and help- ful love of Christ in his home relationships, his feelings and behavior are more likely to respond to his emotional experience than to intellectual instruction, even though daily family devotions be conducted.

Likewise, if a church hopes to develop Christian "response-ability" through its church schools and other functions of church life, it will have to be concerned about the psychological climate of its group life as well as its teachings. (Pp. 97, 98)

Types of Group Leadership

Because the quality or spirit of any group, including that of a church school class, is determined largely by the nature of its leadership, it will be well to consider what kind of class leader a Christian teacher should strive to be.

There are many different kinds of leaders. The autocratic leader sees himself in a position of authority which he may exert and impose on others. He tends to dominate the group, to speak with authority, to think he must know all the answers and make all decisions for the group. He is a military type of commander who gives assignments and expects them to be carried out. He sees himself (and usually places himself) at the head of the group and usually does most of the talking. His predominant role is that of a policeman and a boss, a disciplinarian and a "teller of what to think and do."

Then there is the irresponsible leader who has the responsibility and authority to lead but fails to do so for various reasons. He may be neglecting and shifting his responsibility because he is unprepared to lead or feels inadequate or perhaps just doesn't care what happens. He may be operating under the assumption that the best way to lead a group is to do nothing beyond serving as a "front" for the group or as a class starter. In any case, this kind of leadership often results in a rather aimless, shallow group activity or in someone within the class "taking over" the leadership.

In America today the ideal group leader is seen as one who fulfills a facilitating, helpful, enabling role. We call this type a "democratic" leader because his way of operating leads to democratic group structures and procedures rather than to a dictatorial process. Democracy is a way of life in which all members of a group participate in the development of the values and procedures that govern the group.

What are some of the characteristics of good (productive) group leadership, whether in a classroom or in some other human organization? In recent years many books have been published on this subject. We can only summarize some of the findings under two major principles:

1. A good leader is sensitive to the emotional needs of every individual in the group. Such a teacher is concerned about the feeling of acceptance that every pupil must experience in order to "open up to" and "enter into" the lessons. Motivated by the love of Christ, who sacrificed Himself in order that not one little human being should perish, the Christian teacher is equipped to respect the individual pupil as a child of God loved by God. This basic respect and acceptance, so much a part of true Christian spirit, leads the teacher to be generous and positive and even "permissive" rather than rigid and severe in his relations with his pupils. Such a relationship gives the pupils a feeling of adequacy and freedom of expression.

2. A good leader is an *enabling* person — a stimulator, a counselor, a helper. He encourages a maximum of self-direction, but

sets the stage for learning and planning, furnishes ideas and resources as a stimulus, and guides the group members in the use of their resources. Instead of being a nonparticipant on the one hand or a dictator on the other, a democratic leader or teacher helps the individuals in his group to develop their own competencies and to work together as a group. Jesus said several times: "Whosoever will be great among you shall be your minister" (one who serves others), and this applies also to teachers.

Conditions That Affect Group Spirit

Interwoven with the kind of leadership that encourages healthy and strong group life at any age level are many other factors or conditions. Again we can mention only the major considerations briefly.

1. *The Group Situation*

Physical settings have their effects on the spirit and activities of a group. The size and shape of the room in which the class meets, the acoustics, the color of the walls, the lighting, the temperature, the proportion of space to the size of the group, the space between groups — all of these and many other details are factors in what might be called the atmosphere of the classroom. Certain branches of psychology emphasize that everything in a given "field" or setting is a dynamic that either facilitates or hinders the purposes and spiritual movement of the group. Not all facilities facilitate.

Also the size of a group can be a hindrance to effectiveness. Studies of group functioning suggest that as a group grows beyond 20 members, effective group action becomes increasingly difficult, and that five to seven is a preferred number for full participation. In Sunday school work a single figure cannot be set as the desirable class size, because the age of the pupils, the nature of their activities, and the ability of the teacher enter into the question. But there is good reason to consider dividing any Nursery class of more than 6 (4 present), any Kindergarten-

Primary class of more than 8 (6 present), and a middle or upper grade class of more than 10 (8 present). Even on the youth and adult levels the advantages of a small face-to-face group of 6 to 8 active members are worth considering when other conditions permit such groupings.

The arrangement of the seating is also important. For effective participation the group members must be able to see and hear one another, and the position of the teacher must be conducive to good teacher-class relations. The teacher who sits on the level of the class and within the group is more likely to have direct communication with the group than the teacher who formally stands behind a lectern or sits behind a desk some distance away from the pupils. This physical closeness is especially important in teaching young children. Furthermore, a circular or rectangular seating arrangement in which the teacher is a part of the group tones him down as the center of group communication and encourages interaction within the group.

2. *Group Attitudes*

Much more important than the atmosphere of a group setting and seating arrangement is the atmosphere created by the attitudes of the group. What helps to develop positive, wholesome, creative attitudes? In addition to the kind of leadership already mentioned, three other ingredients in particular seem to be essential to spiritually educative group activity:

a. It is held generally that if a group has common group goals in which all the members are interested, then everyone in the group will become involved in the group process. The goals which a class formulates, or at least becomes aware of and accepts, give its members a sense of purpose, expectation, worthwhileness, and responsibility. Even Nursery children get more interested and excited when they are consulted on a program of activity planned for them.

Goals are usually more challenging and stimulating when they are presented to the group as a *problem*. It is in looking together at a question, in exploring and pooling information and sharing experiences and ideas, that group members are most likely to become interested and involved in a task, whether the task is one of learning or doing. This is especially true when *differing* or even *opposing* insights and desires are permitted and weighed in open discussion and planning.

b. A second distinct quality of good group spirit is friendly informality and a climate of love and warmth. What makes a social atmosphere friendly? We have already said that the leader's manner of behavior and his relationships to the group influence the group perhaps more than any other factor. Classes tend to take on the attitudes of their teachers.

As group members become sensitive to one another's feelings, respectful of the rights and differences of others, forgiving and accepting, feelings of worth and security and pleasure are experienced by the group members in their relations and activities with one another. This attitude in both the leader and the group welcomes the newcomer, encourages participation, and prevents individuals from monopolizing a conversation or task. It is appreciative of everyone's contributions and supports teamwork and the interests of the group as a whole. Pupils who feel neglected and rejected or just tolerated will not respond and participate in class activity as will those who feel respected and encouraged and helped.

c. Also a sense of freedom — freedom to be honest, freedom to participate in a uniquely individual way, freedom to express personal thoughts and feelings — is needed if human beings are to say what they truly think and feel. When pupils are afraid to speak the truth of their own hearts for one reason or another, no amount of urging will generate a flow of response. Regimentation develops a rigid group. Pupils who feel pushed around aren't likely to get as full a measure of the Spirit of God as those who feel loved. Nor are they likely to express the Holy Spirit in such a situation. Cold formality also freezes a group.

This principle of freedom suggests much that will be said

about the kinds of methods of teaching that not only permit but call for participation of all the members of a class on a deeply personal level. Teacher-dominated class procedures inhibit pupil expression and genuine learning. More active and responsible participation or sharing of all the members in a class process leads to greater vitality in the faith and life of the church.

Furthering the Group Process

In addition to the democratic principles of group life and methods of involving pupils in learning activities (discussed in Chapter 6), there are a number of administrative practices which will help a teacher to further the group process in his class.

Among the devices for checking on the quality of the spirit or life of a class is the use of a class observer. This could be the supervisor of instruction, an associate teacher, or an appointed member of the class. In the Appendix are instruments by which an observer can record his observations of the kind of leadership role a particular teacher tends to express; also the extent and nature of class activities during an actual session. The flow chart, on which the number and direction of individual responses in a discussion can be recorded, indicates visually the participation of each class member and the role the leader played. By discussing seriously and without embarrassment the findings of an observer, both a teacher and a class can learn much that might improve their teaching and learning procedures.

Lesson observation sheets might be used by a teacher also for self-examination. The sample in the Appendix looks at the role of the leader and the activity of the group both in the learning of a Bible story or text and also in the activities for learning the lesson truth. By recording a session with a tape recorder or just reflecting on a recent session, a teacher can get many cues on the kind of teaching-learning process which actually takes place in his classroom.

Another way of evaluating the life and progress of a class is to discuss it periodically with the class members or with a small steering committee whose membership can be rotated to include all members over the course of a year. Is the leader doing too much talking? Are certain members participating in the learning activities most of the time, while others merely sit and listen or seem uninterested? Are the activities beyond the abilities of some members? Or are they too simple to interest others? What other reasons might there be for lack of interest?

Occasionally it is revealing to use a simple evaluation or reaction questionnaire with the entire class at the close of a session. Asking the members of the class to indicate their feelings and ideas gives the teacher information that even a sensitive observer may not see. Are the members of the class saying what they actually think? Especially on the upper grade, youth, and adult levels such a reaction sampling can serve to give the group a voice in class planning.

A Concluding Reminder

Christian education is intended to contribute to the development of Christian persons — "the perfecting of the saints." This task requires the nurturing of individuals who are committed to their Lord and Savior Jesus Christ by baptism and faith but who need to become Christian in all dimensions of their lives.

Lutherans have emphasized the doctrine of the means of grace and the role of the Word, especially the verbal word, in Christian education. Without denying the primary role of the Holy Scriptures as the source and norm of Christian faith and life, Christian teachers must recognize also the necessity of relationships and procedures that are conducive to the planting and growth of that Word in the minds and hearts and lives of their pupils.

REVIEW QUESTIONS

1. How would you describe a teacher who sees himself in a facilitating, helping relationship to his class?

2. What physical conditions may affect the spirit of a group?

3. What effect do purposes and expectations have on the spiri[t] of a group?

4. Why is a sense of freedom very important in Christian education?

5. Why is group participation and interaction desirable in any learn-ing activity?

6. What are some ways of checking on the extent and nature of pupil participation in a class session?

CHAPTER SIX

TEACHING METHODS
AND TECHNIQUES

Focus of the chapter: **A general survey of teaching methods — conversation and discussion, group work methods, telling methods, showing methods — and the use of teaching aids, particularly the Bible and basic study course materials.** Reading time: about 20 minutes.

Many people in the church evidently think it doesn't matter *how* the teachers of the church teach, just so *what* they say isn't obviously false.

Undoubtedly the "what," or content, of Christian teaching is of first importance. The seed of Christian faith and life is the Word of God. Unless good seed is planted, the best conditions and methods of farming produce little more than weeds. If the Word of God isn't taught, the saving and sanctifying Spirit and power of God is going to be missing in the process.

But the *way* in which the Word of God is communicated also facilitates or hinders the purposes and work of God. So the "how" of teaching is equally important. Everything we might do to make the message of God's love in Christ meaningful and fruitful to the learner is *method*. There are many methods of teaching and learning.

Which methods are best? This is a question that can be determined only by one's purposes and principles and by specific circumstances. Many principles were indicated in the previous chapters. Furthermore, the church school materials (the basic courses of study and related resources) determine to a large extent the methods used by the teachers of the materials. But the teacher who knows many methods is more equipped to teach skillfully and interestingly and effectively than the one who is limited to a single pattern.

Sharing and Doing Methods

Because pupil participation is considered utterly necessary for good teaching, the modern teacher gives much thought to group methods or ways of involving the pupils in learning activities and tries to avoid talking "at" the pupils. What are some methods of stimulating *group* thinking and *group* activity?

1. *Small Group Discussion*

One of the most common and useful ways of involving pupils in learning and doing is to engage them in conversation and discussion. Discussion is not simply a formal question-and-answer method by which the teacher asks prepared fact questions and the pupils give "correct" answers. A more spiritually significant procedure is to raise questions and problems which the class members themselves can consider, explore, debate, weigh, and conclude.

For a democratic group discussion or conversation the art of questioning is vital. When is a question provocative? What makes a poor question? If the pupils are to think and personally commit themselves to an issue and challenge of life, obviously the following types of questions aren't worth much:

a. Questions that have an obvious answer, such as "Does Jesus love everybody?" or "Does Jesus hate anybody?"

b. Questions that may be debatable but which are so presented that there is obviously only one answer the leader will accept; e. g., "What should all people confess?"

c. Questions that call for factual answers which the group simply doesn't know; e. g., "What happened in 1054 A. D.?" or "What kind of fish did the disciples eat?"

d. Questions containing big words that the pupils do not understand; e. g., "How would you explain Christocentric-dynamic theory?"

e. Vague questions, such as "What happens when we sin?"

f. Questions that may be answered yes or no; for instance, "Was Martha a friend of Jesus?"

The most stimulating questions permit "open-ended" rather than fixed answers, respect the learner's ability to think, call for personal reflection and opinion, and frequently refer to the personal experiences and feelings of the pupils; e. g., "How do you feel about your Sunday school?" or "What does belonging to God mean to you?"

This kind of discussion is facilitated by small circular or rectangular groupings, as was indicated in Chapter 5, and can be conducted also in larger classes through "buzz groups" or small "huddles." In this method, two to six pupils are asked to consider a question as a subcommittee and then to report to the total group.

2. *The Workshop Way*

Workshop procedure is similar to the committee discussion method, but it is more organized and calls for more than a quick response. It involves assignments to individual members of the committee, work between sessions of the group, and the use of resource materials and resource persons. This more extensive and penetrating study of a work group usually is reported to the entire class or at least to the instructor in a formal presentation — a paper, a report, a recommendation, a demonstration, etc. Also young children enjoy preparing something at home for the next lesson. The symposium by which three or four participants present their findings or points of view on a subject is another form in which reporting can take place especially in classes for older pupils. The entire class can be involved by having an open forum follow a committee presentation.

3. *Interviews and Panels*

A panel discussion differs from a symposium or simple group discussion in that the panel members usually face the audience and the moderator poses leading questions that call for an exchange of ideas. In a sense it is a group interview. In like manner, individuals in a class can be interviewed by the instructor or a member of the class or in an open hearing. Permitting the group to react and comment heightens group participation and interest.

4. *Brainstorming and the Circular Response*

These techniques of getting pupil response make use of the free association of ideas. In brainstorming the leader simply calls on the group members to say whatever "flashes" into their minds in reference to a given question or problem. No one needs to ask for the floor. The ideas need not make sense. The spontaneous responses are usually recorded and then grouped and evaluated by the class.

For a circular response the leader suggests that each member of the group express himself on the subject, starting anywhere in the group and proceeding to the next person until all have had their say.

5. *Dramatics and Role Playing*

There are, of course, many types of dramatics. With young children, informal playing of a Bible story or its lesson not only involves the pupils but stirs their imagination and gives practice in living out the lesson truth. More formal plays, tableaux, pageants, programs, pantomimes, use of puppets, etc., can engage older children also in the development of the scripts.

With a growing interest in the emotional life of the pupils

has come a growing use of role playing as an educational method. Sometimes called sociodrama or psychodrama, depending on whether the problem is chiefly social or individual, role playing is a spontaneous acting out of a situation or conflict and helps the actor to understand his own emotions or the viewpoints and feelings of others.

For example, members of a class might take turns playing the role of a teacher who has just had an upsetting disturbance in the class. The role playing would then demonstrate how class members would handle the problem while it deepens in them the awareness of the problem and sympathetic concern about it.

6. *Workbook, Handwork, and "Creative" Activities*

The use of workbook exercises, handwork, tests, questionnaires, reading and research assignments, and an endless variety of art media of expression can be seen as individual activity rather than as group process. They are lumped together here in order to limit the number of categories.

Even though paper-and-pencil activities and predesigned "handwork" tend to be carried out on a rather matter-of-fact level, they can be useful in establishing background and are often a starting point for discussion. The coloring of an outline drawing, the making of a paper model, or the use of tests and "exercises" with elementary school children can serve to focus attention on a Bible event or truth.

More important are so-called "creative" activities, in which the pupils are encouraged to express their own responses to God's Word in a great variety of forms. When pupils are given opportunity to "relate" their own thoughts and feelings to the Word and Spirit of God in verbal compositions, art projects, and social actions, Christian nurture becomes richer and learning is more likely to become experience "in depth." This kind of doing is application of the Word in a personal, functional sense, a much more effective type of application than a pious admonition that isn't put into the stream of the learner's life.

Telling and Showing Methods

Our prior presentation of group methods does not imply that the telling methods — lecture, storytelling, preaching in the Biblical sense of Gospel proclamation — have little place in Christian education today. When telling is combined with showing and group members participate with active interest and thoughtful listening, the lecture method is often more meaningful and educational than other types of activities. But telling and showing methods require preparation and skill to be effective.

1. *Storytelling*

"They All Love a Story" is the title of an article that appeared in *Interaction,* a magazine that church school teachers will find worth reading regularly.* This observation applies especially to young children, but it is also true of older youth, young people, and adults if they haven't heard the story and if it's told well.

Good Bible storytelling begins with prayerful and thorough preparation, a clear understanding of the purpose of the story, and awareness of the needs of the pupils to whom the story is to be told. It demands the ability to tell the story freely without being tied to a written or memorized version. Storytelling is enhanced by the use of direct speech, role playing by the teller, and by appropriate facial expressions and bodily movements.

The Bible story gains educational point and purpose when it is introduced with an "approach." A review of related incidents recently studied, the raising of a question, a reference to some current event, the showing of a picture or object or any other means of readying the group for the attentive hearing of the story will serve to highlight the significance of the story.

Though points of application or personal reference may be made in the course of the story itself, it is usually best to leave the meaning of the story and its application to the discussion

* Doris Graesser, "They All Love a Story," *Interaction,* II, 11 (August 1962), 2—6.

which can follow the conclusion of the story proper. The use of the review and application pictures which are often included in the printed lesson materials will aid in sustaining interest in this phase of the storytelling method.

An observation sheet for evaluating storytelling (Appendix A) calls attention to two major concerns: the story structure and the manner of presentation. Questions about the structure deal with the approach, the transition, the story proper, the review questions, the application. The presentation can be examined in terms of body movements, voice and speed, the dramatizing of the story, and the attention of the group.

2. *Use of Teaching Aids*

Ordinarily the most helpful teaching aid is the basic course of study with its graded materials for departmental worship, its leader's and teacher's guides, and pupil's leaflets or study books. The teacher of any age group, adult as well as preschool, is bound to have unnecessary work or aimlessness if he ventures to teach without using studiously some carefully prepared lesson materials as the basis for his lessons. Every major church denomination in America prepares and publishes such lesson materials with good reason, and the teacher who teaches "on his own" does so at great risk and with a grave responsibility.

How to use printed lesson helps wisely is a subject that will be considered in the following chapter. Here we are simply noting the principle that printed lesson materials are helpful tools when used properly. Of course, materials of any kind are only means and not ends in themselves. They are "helps," or aids, and must not be followed slavishly or come between a teacher and his pupils. But they do furnish content and directions and activities that the ordinary teacher does not have the experience, time, and resources to prepare.

Correlated with or available as supplementary to basic course materials are many types of audio-visual aids. The use of one or the other of these media is a type of showing method usually combined with one or more other methods.

Among the more commonly used visual materials in religious education are flat pictures, charts, maps, models, blackboard outlines and drawings, flannelboards, objects, dioramas, puppets, murals, bulletin boards, room decorations, filmstrips, and motion pictures. Demonstrations, dramatics, field trips, and exhibits also are ways of showing a lesson.

Because the use of the eye-gate as well as the ear-gate steps up attention and learning, this subject deserves extensive study by the church school teacher. Regular use of showing methods contributes to good teaching, unless, of course, other principles of teaching are violated.

3. *Use of the Bible*

A most important showing method is the use of the Bible. Leading children into the Bible is not just another way of stimulating pupil activity and interest. It is that, but at the same time the use of the Bible relates the pupil to the Book of books, gives the pupil a firsthand visual impression of God's Word, and makes use of the reading method, which studies have indicated results in more learning than the simple telling method. At the same time the regular use of the Bible in the classroom develops habits of Bible reading and familiarity with the Bible as a book.

Regardless of the age level being taught, every lesson in a church school can include some reference to the Bible book itself. The preschool teacher can use it as a visual symbol and demonstrate its use by opening it as the source of her Bible story or memory words. From third grade on up (Junior level), every pupil needs a Bible of his own and can be trained to bring it to class and to use it — in class and at home. In youth and adult Bible classes the Bible ought to be the main textbook. On these levels the course material becomes the guide for the study of the Bible text itself.

REVIEW QUESTIONS

1. What are some of the advantages of sharing and doing methods?

2. What kind of questions are most likely to stimulate group discussion? What kind are to be avoided?

3. What are the values of the storytelling method? Mention some of the ground rules in the use of this method.

4. How many different kinds of audio-visual aids can you mention? In what ways can they aid teaching and learning?

5. In what way do printed lesson helps aid teachers in selecting methods of teaching?

6. What opportunities for using the Bible present themselves in the Sunday school hour? What values are there in the use of the Bible itself?

CHAPTER SEVEN

PREPARING TO
TEACH A LESSON

Focus of the chapter: **Principles of lesson planning, the function of purpose in the preparation
of a lesson, the purposeful use of the teacher's
guide and the pupil's materials, and a mode of
developing a lesson plan.** Reading time: about
25 minutes.

Even teachers who know why they teach, what to teach, and how
to teach need to plan each individual lesson carefully and thought-
fully. Especially is this true in the church school which has very
limited time for accomplishing its spiritual tasks of eternal importance. There is no other way to worthwhile lessons except
through preparation, even though teaching plans may have to be
modified in the classroom. Good planning allows for changes in
procedure to meet the needs and interests of the pupils.

It is possible to teach a church school lesson with very little
preparation. Many teachers do just that. They simply read or
repeat more or less what is in the lesson printed for the pupils
and direct their pupils to the printed questions and memory words
and exercises. But the teaching of subject matter which has not
been distilled and assimilated by the teacher through personal
study is not likely to be organized, interesting, properly graded,
and richly relevant to the needs of the pupils. Nor is it likely to

communicate the Spirit of God, who usually works most effectively in a spiritual relationship and interaction between teachers and learners.

Lesson Planning Procedures

In a broad sense all the concerns considered in previous chapters are a part of a teacher's preparation for teaching a specific lesson. Awareness of general objectives, a broad acquaintance with the curriculum and its related materials, some understanding of the pupils, and at least a minimum of training and experience in group leadership and teaching techniques — these are basic preparations, as is the development of the teacher's own Christian faith and life. But here the question is the preparation of a specific lesson.

The first rule of procedure important to thorough lesson planning is *"Begin early."* The teacher who waits until Sunday morning to look at the lesson for the day can't begin to uncover the depths of its meaning, to select and try out the most suitable activities, to explore and gather together the available resources, and to relate the lesson to current events and the personal lives of the pupils. The teacher who studies and is aware of a lesson for some days in advance of teaching it and attends a staff meeting at which the lesson is discussed discovers all kinds of related ideas that would otherwise not pop up to enrich the lesson.

A second rule of procedure is *"Pray."* Only the teacher who cares enough to pray, who feels his inadequacies for the task and seeks in spirit the help of God, who in love of God and for the welfare of the pupils implores the guidance and blessing of God, is going to be led and assisted by God to prepare as well as possible. And those who pray have the promise of Jesus, "Ask and it shall be given unto you; seek and ye shall find; knock and it shall be opened unto you." (Matt. 7:7; Luke 11:9)

A third general rule to follow in preparing to teach a Bible lesson is this: *"Begin with the Bible"* and the study of the Biblical basis of the lesson. The Holy Scriptures are the revelation of God, and the Word of God is the means of grace and the norm of Christian life for teachers as well as pupils. To be prepared to teach the Bible, a teacher must be a Bible student. Direct personal study of the Bible will give teachers of the church insights and convictions and a power they will not get otherwise.

Before studying the teacher's guide or the pupil's book, before deciding on any activity, first read the proposed Scripture passage in the Bible, compare it with some other translation, look at the context and parallel passages, and do some original, personal thinking about it. These three questions are often recommended as a guide for textual study: What does it say? What does it mean? What does it say to me and my students?

Not until a teacher is fairly familiar with the Biblical text of the lesson and its central theme, thought, truth, or doctrine is he ready to plan how to further the learning of the lesson.

The Purposeful Use of Materials

To help teachers in their study of the lesson and in the preparation of a teaching plan, most church denominations publish teaching guides or manuals. The Concordia teachers quarterlies provide some commentary on the Biblical text for the various Sunday lessons and suggest the aim or desired outcome of the lesson and the truth or emphasis by means of which the specific goal is to be approached.

A clear understanding and statement of the goal (aim or purpose) of the lesson is needed for good lesson planning as well as for good teaching. It is purpose that gives a lesson direction and meaning and value, enables a teacher to organize a lesson with proper emphasis, and determines the appropriateness of the selected learning activities. Significant learning is more likely to result when there is awareness and acceptance of the purpose of a lesson on the part of both pupils and teacher.

When either the teacher or the pupils feel that a lesson or some part of it is pointless, there will be lack of interest and little or no application to life.

Having determined the purpose of the lesson, the teacher is ready to examine the pupil's leaflet or study book and the teaching suggestions in the teachers quarterly in terms of content and activities that will serve the specific purpose. Of course, a teacher can follow the pupil's text, the lesson helps, and the teachers quarterly rigidly in complete disregard of the needs and interests of the pupils, or he can neglect them completely. Neither use of printed lesson helps is wise.

But lesson helps can be valuable aids to personal lesson planning and teaching. They furnish directions and suggestions from specialists who give much more time and experienced attention to the preparation of the printed materials than the ordinary volunteer teacher can devote to lesson planning. They deserve, therefore, to be studied and used regularly and conscientiously.

But the quarterlies, leaflets, workbooks, visual aids, and activity materials are only aids — tools — resources — helps. As tools they can help teachers teach and learners to learn, but they can also get in the way of good personal teaching and learning. This happens when prepared materials keep teachers from thinking and planning creatively and when they cause teachers to overlook the needs and interests of their pupils. Prepared materials have value only to the extent to which they help the teacher toward the achievement of goals.

In planning a lesson the teacher needs to examine the printed materials for the pupils along with the teaching guide; the printed lessons are built around the graded theme, usually provide an introduction or approach, and carry pictures that will prove useful. They also include memory verses, hymns, Bible study and discussion questions, and points of application to life. In further reading of the guide or manual the teacher will receive additional suggestions for (1) the approach to the lesson, (2) the basic presentation of Bible content, (3) activities for learning the lesson truth, and (4) ways to conclude the class period and to extend the lesson beyond the session.

Constructing a Lesson Plan

To get the most out of advance study of a lesson and lesson materials, it is strongly recommended that teachers write out their lesson plans in one form or another. Experienced teachers may get by with some brief notes and a time schedule, but beginning teachers will find a rather complete outline of the lesson and a tentative schedule of activities nearly indispensable to success. On pages 65 and 66 is a detailed lesson-plan outline and an illustration of what might be done.

The first part of the sample lesson plan calls for a study of the Biblical content of the lesson, its educational purpose, and its relevance to the lives of the pupils. The last point in this section requires some reflection as to what the related interests and needs of the pupils might be. What questions may have been asked but not sufficiently answered on the previous Sunday? What events that may have some bearing on the lesson have occurred during the week? What individual experience has some pupil had that may illustrate the point of the lesson?

The second half of the plan requires preparation of specific procedures for teaching the lesson. It divides the class session into four major parts: (1) the beginning, (2) activities for learning the story (or what the Bible says), (3) activities for learning the lesson truth, and (4) the close.

The introduction (formerly called the approach) is the point of contact which deserves special planning. It serves to catch the interest of the class and to focus attention on the central theme or truth. The methods of lesson study proper are seen as learning activities requiring pupil participation. The activities focus first on learning the Bible story or selection and then on learning the application or lesson truth. Such planning makes

MY SUNDAY SCHOOL LESSON PLAN FOR _____

Class _____ Teacher _____

Bible Story or Content and Reference — Flight to Egypt, Matt. 2:13-23

Review of Previous Lesson(s) — In searching for Jesus the Wise Men from the East had stopped in Jerusalem and inquired of Herod where the newborn King of the Jews might be found.

Notes on the Bible Story (or Text)

Historical Setting (When and Where)
> This event is a consequence of the visit of the Wise Men. It took place in Bethlehem. King Herod had encouraged the Wise Men to find the child Jesus and to report back to him. When Herod saw that he had been tricked, he became very angry.

Characters (Who)
> Wise Men, Herod, angel, Joseph and Mary, Jesus

Brief Story or Textual Outline (What)
> Wise Men see star while in the East
> They inquire in Jerusalem
> They find Jesus and are warned
> God's angel appears to Joseph
> The holy family flees to Egypt
> Herod orders the infants of Bethlehem murdered
> The holy family returns to Palestine

Interesting Details in the Lesson Notes
> Wise Men and Joseph probably fled the same night.
> Dec. 28 is the day set aside in the church year for the remembrance of the Holy Innocents. Number of children slain was perhaps about a dozen.

Desired Outcome (Why)
> That the children may trust in their heavenly Father's care at all times.

Specific Age-Level Theme or Emphasis (Point or Aim)
> Being in God's care, we need not be afraid in darkness or danger.

Related Experiences and Questions and Lesson Applications

How did God take care of the babies who were killed?
Could God save you in an airplane crash or in an atomic war?
When do children often become afraid?
How can we be sure of God's care?

My Procedures for Teaching This Lesson	Time Allowed

How I Plan to Begin 5 minutes

Show picture of a boy who seems to be afraid and ask class members to tell what they think is happening.

Activities for Learning the Bible Story Well 15 minutes

1. Have class as a whole outline the story and tell the incidents.
2. Check Bible reference questions about the story and use the test — Exercise B.

Activities for Learning the Lesson Truth 10 minutes

1. Discuss the "Learning the Truth" exercise.
2. Study the cartoon in the lesson book and have pupils picture God's care in a drawing of their own.

Related Materials (Teaching Aids and Resources)

Pictures of angels watching over God's children — from picture file.

How I Might Extend the Lesson Through the Week 5 minutes

Have pupils make a survey of whether people still believe in angels. Try to find an unusual story about God's care of His children today.

How I Plan to Close 5 minutes

Talk about New Year's resolutions of people saved by God for His purposes. Drill memory words. Prayer of dedication by a pupil.

Teacher's Signature _____

teaching much more than mere presentation by the teacher and relates learning to the life of the pupils. The closing assignments serve to individualize teaching and learning and extend the lesson into the days that follow.

To avoid an unbalanced session in which most of the time available is used up in prolonged introductory discussion or in the telling of the story or in drill and recitation of memory words, a teacher must adjust the session plan to the length of the lesson period. Roughly scheduling the time for the various parts of the lesson plan will help to keep the planned lesson moving on Sunday morning. Regular review of the schedule and a weighing of the relative values of the class activities will help teachers make the most of their time.

Evaluation

Evaluation of all aspects of a lesson soon after it has been taught will serve to improve lesson planning. What seemed to click? What were the trouble spots? Did the lesson serve its purpose or was the main point lost along the way? What might I have done differently and perhaps better? These and similar questions, if reflected on shortly after a session, will lead to better planning and teaching.

Even more helpful is a periodic evaluation by someone else who might objectively observe and then helpfully discuss the teacher's use of his lesson plan. Such an analysis might be made by a supervisor of instruction (the pastor, a minister of education, or a professional public school teacher), or a team teacher, the department superintendent, or simply by a friend. The teacher can listen critically to himself on the basis of a tape recording. The Appendix provides several class observation instruments.

Good teaching is usually a reflection of thorough preparation and good planning. With a plan a teacher knows what he's doing.

REVIEW QUESTIONS

1. What might be some of the values of good lesson planning and therefore good reasons for advance preparation of lessons?

2. Mention at least three preliminary *procedures* for thoughtful lesson planning.

3. How can one best discover the *meanings* of a given Biblical selection?

4. What are some of the effects that clear purposes may produce in planning and teaching?

5. How would you describe the best use of prepared lesson helps?

6. What definite teaching procedures should be listed in a written lesson plan?

CHAPTER EIGHT

CONCERNS BEYOND
THE CLASSROOM

Focus of the chapter: **The need for a pastoral concern for each individual pupil, what some of these pastoral activities of a Christian teacher might be, and opportunities for ongoing leadership training and in-service growth.** Reading time: about 20 minutes.

Way back in Chapter 3 we said: "Though a teacher is not the pastor of an entire congregation, a Christian teacher must also be a pastor — a shepherd, an overseer — in the Biblical and functional meaning of the word. He is to care about and care for the souls of the individuals in his care. The concern of the church and of its teachers is the perfecting of the saints, the nurturing of spiritual growth toward Christian maturity in those who receive the righteousness and Spirit of Christ by faith. This means that what a pupil does outside the classroom is as much a concern of the Christian teacher as what a pupil says and does in the class — perhaps more so."

Also in the classroom the teacher who is seriously concerned about the spiritual life of the pupils will give just as much attention to the *lives* and the *spirit* of his pupils as he gives to prepared lessons and lesson plans. The latter are indeed helpful, but they are only means, tools, aids which ought to serve the spiritual needs

69

of the pupils in a very personal way. The pupils, we must remember, are individuals — persons with thoughts and feelings of their own. And though spiritual learning is wholly dependent on the grace and Spirit of God, the miracle and mystery of regeneration and Christian growth cannot take place unless the individual pupils receive the Word and Spirit of God into their own minds and hearts and lives.

Genuine spiritual nurture therefore calls for a pastoral concern for each individual pupil, and this kind of concern for the spiritual life of the individual makes demands which are beyond those of a given lesson or class session. This chapter looks at some of these responsibilities beyond the classroom.

The Teacher as Evangelist

In this book not much has been said about evangelism, but rightly understood, it is inherent in the work of Christian education. God wants all men (and women and children — also in your community) saved and therefore "to come unto the knowledge of the truth" (1 Tim. 2:4). In order that the church might teach and make disciples and nurture children, youth, and adults in the Lord, outreach is necessary. People, young and old, must be brought into regular contact with the Word. "How shall they believe in Him of whom they have not heard?" asks Paul. (Rom. 10:14)

Thus every Christian, but particularly the teacher of the church, has the task of evangelism first of all in the narrow sense of the term — that of reaching out to the unchurched in order that they might be taught, of going out to bring them into a Gospel teaching program, and of supporting the missionary programs of the church. Since the pupils, too, are to serve their Lord by being witnesses of Christ and going out to find His lost lambs and sheep, they must be motivated and directed in this work. Basic for this stimulation is a strong program of mission education and planned occasions and projects for mission work.

But evangelism is more than a program of outreach — of canvassing, of making contacts, of bringing someone to Sunday school and church, of getting others to add names to the church rolls, and of giving an offering for missions. In the deeper meaning of the word, it is the evangelizing of people, which requires teaching the Evangel, or Gospel, of Jesus Christ and communicating His Spirit. As indicated previously, the church's evangelizing, Christianizing power is in the Spirit of God working through the teaching and learning of the Gospel.

In America we call the teaching of the Gospel "Christian education"; in Europe Christian educators prefer to call all their teaching "evangelism." This latter practice emphasizes the fact that teaching is truly Christian only when it is Gospel preaching and teaching, that is, when it serves to relate people to God and nourishes Christian faith through the Gospel of God's redemptive acts of love in Jesus Christ.

But because this work of evangelizing people is often oversimplified in the use of the term evangelism, we might well continue to designate the church's teaching activities as Christian education or Christian nurture as long as we understand this work as evangelism in the broad sense. Needed for this point of view is also the understanding that the Gospel in the broad sense is more than mere historical incidents in the life of Jesus. It is even more than the fundamental truth of God's love and forgiveness. In the broad sense it is the whole Word of God speaking to the whole life of a person about life in relationship to God.

The true Gospel teacher has the task of teaching "all the counsel of God" (Acts 20:27; Matt. 28:20), but of doing so with a deep concern for personal commitment and responses to God's Word and Spirit on the part of each individual pupil, especially outside the classroom. In other words, the Christian teacher is to "do the work of an evangelist" (2 Tim. 4:5), urging faith in Jesus Christ as Lord and Savior and faithfulness to God in all things out of grateful appreciation of His goodness, His love, His salvation, His blessings received so freely through Jesus Christ.

71

The Teacher as Counselor

Essential to this task of relating the entire life of the individual pupil to Christ and His Word is the teacher's role as a friend and counselor. Spiritual teaching deals with the spirit and life of the individual. It involves talking privately to a boy who needs comfort over the loss of his father, giving a kind explanation to someone who asks a disturbing question, listening patiently to a person with a problem, conferring with individuals or a class on learning or behavior problems.

Much of this work may go on outside the class period — in a presession conversation, during the informal moments at the beginning or close of a lesson, between Sunday school and church, and on chance meetings during the week. Mark Soderly was a young teen-ager who usually was polite and cooperative and helpful. When the rest of the class became inattentive and disturbing, he often would call them to order for the sake of Mrs. Creighton, who sometimes let things get out of hand. One particular Sunday, however, Mark was noticeably upset. He argued with anything Mrs. Creighton said, fought with the kids around him, ate candy during the lesson, and kept banging his chair on the floor. In talking to Mark after class, Mrs. Creighton discovered that she had started the trouble on the previous Sunday by repeatedly calling Mark her dear boy in front of the others.

Personal contacts that are arranged also serve to establish helpful relationships between teachers and pupils and further a Christian teacher's influence. A teacher who visits his pupils in their homes gets to know the parents and the home life of the pupils. Such visits also serve to remind parents of their primary responsibility in the Christian instruction and training of their children and youth. They furthermore stimulate parental support of the church school program in general and the teacher's endeavors in particular. One Sunday school recently reported scheduled interviews with parents at the church. Interviews with individual pupils would also prove rewarding.

Taking the pupils on field trips or arranging social projects for them and with them is another way of entering with Christ into their lives more fully. A high school Bible class teacher didn't begin to enjoy his teaching, nor did he feel he was getting anywhere with his class of boys, until he began taking along two or three of them at a time on some of his business trips. His students told him more about themselves while traveling with him in a car for a few hours than he could have ever learned in any other way.

The Teacher as Teacher

Every Sunday school teacher (or any other kind of church school teacher) is called to be not only an evangelist and a counselor but also preeminently a *teacher* of the church. An official, public teacher of the church (whether volunteer or professional) has the responsibility to teach the teachings of Scripture and nothing contrary to its doctrines, to carry out conscientiously the prescribed program of instruction adopted by those in authority (he hasn't the right to teach whatever he pleases), and he is to represent his local congregation in relating the pupils to the life of the parish. In the broad but very real meaning of the word, he is a minister or servant of the church as well as of God and the pupils.

The teacher who is genuinely interested in the spiritual development of his pupils will desire also the extension of the lesson beyond the class period. To that end he may make assignments (preferably creative ones for which individual initiative and imagination are needed), and he will frequently challenge the pupils to live out the lesson. He will furthermore show interest in the pupils' through-the-week activities and will check periodically on the daily devotional life of the pupils.

In addition to being concerned about the personal and family devotions in the homes of the pupils, a Christian teacher will do well to encourage and arrange attendance at church worship services — both regular and special. The habit of participation in the worship services of the parish is much more important to the future faith of the pupils than knowing how many times Joshua and his men marched around the walls of Jericho.

Included in the task of relating pupils to the life of the church is the development of their awareness of the church's mission and welfare programs, the observance of the church year and local church activities, the support of the parish's other educational and fellowship programs, and the acquainting of pupils with the church staff (the pastor, minister of education, music director, youth leaders, janitor, Sunday school superintendent, etc.). Pupils are strengthened in their Christian faith and life through vital and meaningful church relationships and a strong identification with a church body and its leaders.

The Teacher as Student

One more concern of a church school teacher deserves consideration. It is the teacher's need for in-service training and personal growth.

Church school teachers have many opportunities for ongoing help. Most parishes have a schedule of local staff meetings, part of which are set aside for the study and preparation of the Sunday lessons. Teachers who regularly attend these meetings grow in knowledge and understanding of God's Word and become better teachers than they would be otherwise. At these meetings, which sometimes begin with Bible study and then break into departmental workshops, on occasion there are also book reviews, the use of teaching films and filmstrips, the discussion of articles in *Interaction,* guest speakers, demonstrations, etc.

At least once if not twice a year many parishes offer a ten-week leadership training course or Bible institute. These courses, too, give teachers an opportunity to become more deeply versed in the Word and more proficient in communicating the Word to others. The Concordia Leadership Training program provides a series of textbooks and instructors' guides which lead to the certifying of lay church school teachers.

The Concordia training courses are grouped into two series, one dealing chiefly with Bible and doctrinal content and one with education and administration. An individual earning four credits (one credit per completed course) is awarded a first certificate, provided that two of the credits are for courses in the first series and two for courses in the second series. Those who complete an additional two courses in each of the two categories are awarded an advanced certificate. Individuals completing twelve courses, six in each category, receive a special award.

"Trained teachers are better teachers." This has been the slogan of the Concordia Leadership Training program for many years. There are various other avenues of training. There are, as further example, the regional, district, and national conferences and conventions. Attendance at such meetings is as important for church school workers as are the conferences of professional people in or out of the church. Participation in such meetings deserves to be taken for granted by all who hold public teaching offices in the church.

One more way of growing as a teacher of the church: reading. Concordia publishes "a monthly magazine church school workers grow by." It's called *Interaction*. Getting and reading it or a similar publication helps to keep a teacher alive to new ideas and fills in some of the gaps in his or her background. The gradual building of a personal library and the use of a church library with an up-to-date section of books on the Bible and Christian education also contributes to the making of teachers who are qualified and able to do their work well.

To young Timothy Paul wrote: "Study [do your best] to show thyself approved unto God [to present yourself to God as one qualified and approved], a workman that needeth not to be ashamed, rightly dividing [or dealing with] the Word of truth" (2 Tim. 2:15). God wants able church workers. By inspiration of God, St. Paul also wrote: "And the things which thou hast heard of me among many witnesses, the same commit thou to faithful men who shall be able to teach others also." (2 Tim. 2:2)

The church of today and tomorrow needs well-trained church school workers more than ever before. You, too, can teach for Christ and His church. But *trained* leaders and teachers make *better* schools, and better, more dedicated and skillful teachers are also happier teachers. Become a better *trained* worker in every way possible, for this is the best way to help the church fulfill its mission and teaching task.

REVIEW QUESTIONS

1. Why is evangelism a necessary part of the church's ministry of teaching?

2. What does it mean to evangelize a person?

3. What are some of the values of an annual visit in the homes of all pupils?

4. Mention several occasions when a teacher might serve as a Christian counselor to his pupils.

5. How can teachers help to relate their pupils to the life of the church?

6. What are the Christian teacher's chief opportunities for in-service training and growth?

SAMPLE OBSERVATION FORM
FOR EVALUATION OF STORYTELLING

1. The Story Structure

   a. How interesting was the approach?

   b. Did the transition have a logical connection?

   c. Was the story complete enough? too detailed?

   d. Were questions about the story answered readily?

   e. How about the application? Appropriate? Too brief?

2. Manner of Presentation

   a. Body position and movements OK?

   b. How about the voice and speed of speech?

   c. Was the story dramatized sufficiently? too much?

   d. Any distractions?

3. Other Comments or Questions

SAMPLE OBSERVATION FORM
FOR EVALUATION OF DISCUSSION

1. Notes on procedure for getting the discussion started.

2. What seemed to help the discussion move along?

3. Number of times each member of the group responded.

4. Difficulties in the material or questions used.

5. Problems of participation that individual members of the group seemed to have.

6. How might one improve the discussion?

SAMPLE OBSERVATION FORM
(Flow Chart)

Chart 1 (leader-dominated group).

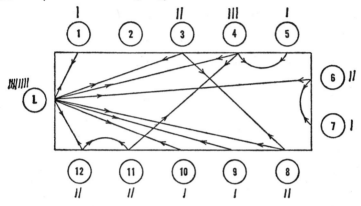

Chart 2 (fairly well-integrated group).

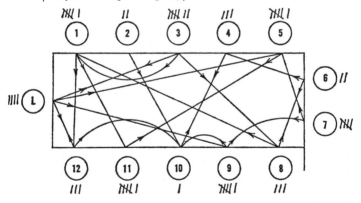

From *Manual for Discussion Leaders and Participants*, by Paul Bergevin and Dwight Morris. Copyright 1955 by Seabury Press. Used by permission.

79

A SUNDAY SCHOOL LESSON PLAN FOR _____

Class _____ Teacher _____

Bible Story or Content and Reference

Review of Previous Lesson(s)

Notes on the Bible Story (or Text)

Historical Setting (When and Where)

Characters (Who)

Brief Story or Textual Outline (What)

Interesting Details in Lesson Notes

Desired Outcome (Why)

Specific Age-Level Theme or Emphasis (Point or Aim)

Related Experiences, Needs, and Interests of Pupils and Lesson Applications

APPENDIX D-1

My Procedures for Teaching This Lesson	Time Allowed

How I Plan to Begin

Activities for Learning the Bible Story Well

Activities for Learning the Lesson Truth

Related Materials (Teaching Aids and Resources)

How I Might Extend the Lesson Through the Week

How I Plan to Close

_____

Teacher's Signature

A CLASS OBSERVATION INSTRUMENT

Identifying Information

1. Date _____

2. Observer's name _____

3. Class observed _____

4. What was going on? _____

5. In what kind of setting? _____

6. Number of pupils present _____

Transmission of Ideas

7. Source and basis of teacher's statements or appeals (check)

_____the Bible

_____the standards of the church

_____the teacher's own beliefs and experiences

_____"what other people think"

_____the judgment of the group

_____what the textbook says or some other "higher authority"

_____the rights and experiences of others

8. Describe what you think the teacher is trying to "put across" to the class.

9. Ways in which the teacher makes his points (applications)

_____"should do"   _____"should not do"

_____"should know"   _____"should not know"

_____"a good thing"   _____"a bad thing"

_____shows meaning   _____calls for interpretation

_____praises for   _____criticizes for

_____refers to Christ   _____uses Gospel to motivate

Group Activity During Class Session

10. Method of participation (check)

    ____listening, looking   ____reporting, demonstrating

    ____discussing, witnessing   ____worshiping, offering

    ____reading, studying   ____trying out, acting out

    ____creating, making   ____being tested, quizzed

    ____drilling, reciting   ____other _____

11. Teacher-class interaction pattern (check one)

    ____All activity is from the teacher toward the group or its members.

    ____All activity is coming from the class and is directed toward the teacher.

    ____The teacher takes up about half of the total interaction time, about as much as all the other group members put together.

    ____The teacher's activity is about as much as the average member.

    ____The teacher is definitely a "participating observer" on the fringe of the group rather than its center.

12. The "discipline" of the class (check one)

    ____Every member of the group just talks up when he feels like it, either to the whole group, the teacher, or to individuals. Considerable confusion and competition for attention results.

    ____Everyone seems to listen or speak in proper place with due respect for others but with no special rules for recognition and no disorder.

    ____Everyone signals the person in charge for recognition before he speaks, but the air is quite informal.

    ____Everyone signals the person in charge in a formal manner when he wishes to speak, and the person in charge handles the situation formally.

    ____Speaking is done only when one is called on. Person in charge may ask who wants to speak, but the procedure is definitely a "calling on" process rather than spontaneous asking for the floor.

13. Intensity of interest in class activity (check one)

    ____Extreme lack of interest — the class members literally daydream, horseplay, turn backs on what is going on, call it "quits."

    ____Boredom, with some restraint expressing itself in yawning, whispering, looking around with some pretense at being interested.

_____Signs of mild lack of interest — smothered yawning, head and leg twisting, eye wandering, relaxed attention.

_____Attentive interest, concentration — shown by posture or actions focused on the activity and enjoyment.

_____Enthusiastic interest — entering into the activity with spirit, all-out participation, and delight.

14. The predominant role played by the teacher during this observation

_____policeman, "keeper in line," disciplinarian

_____"boss," "teller of what to do"

_____teacher, educator, trainer

_____adviser, supervisor, "backer-upper"

_____organizer, manager, chairman

_____comrade, member of the group, equal

_____sideliner, listener, nonparticipant

_____temporarily absent, busy with other activities

Teacher _____

Class _____

Date _____

LESSON OBSERVATION FORM

A. Type of Approach _____

  1. Was it interesting? _____ Why? _____

  _____

  _____

  2. How did the approach lead into or fail to connect with the lesson?

  _____

  _____

  3. Other comments _____

  _____

B. Activities for Learning the Bible Content _____

  _____

The Role of the Leader

  1. Too dominating? _____

  2. Communicated well? _____

  3. Used visual aids? _____

  4. Failed to give sufficient information? _____

  5. Worked at getting pupil participation? _____

The Activity of the Group

  1. Seemed attentive and interested? _____

  2. Contributed information or opinion? _____

  3. Asked questions? _____

  4. Got out of hand? _____

  5. Found the material too difficult? _____ too easy? _____

  6. Used the Bible? _____

C. Activities for Learning the Lesson Truth _____

_____

The Role of the Leader

1. Dominated the procedures? _____

2. Allowed for change of plans? _____

3. Invited participation? _____

4. Functioned as counselor and helper? _____

5. Allowed for individual differences? _____

6. Summarized the theme or lesson truth? _____

The Participation of the Group

1. Contributed opinions and ideas? _____

2. Felt free to disagree? _____

3. Asked for help? _____

4. Was more active than passive? _____

5. Respected the rights of others? _____